100 Years Enriching Lives:

Family and Consumer Sciences at UGA

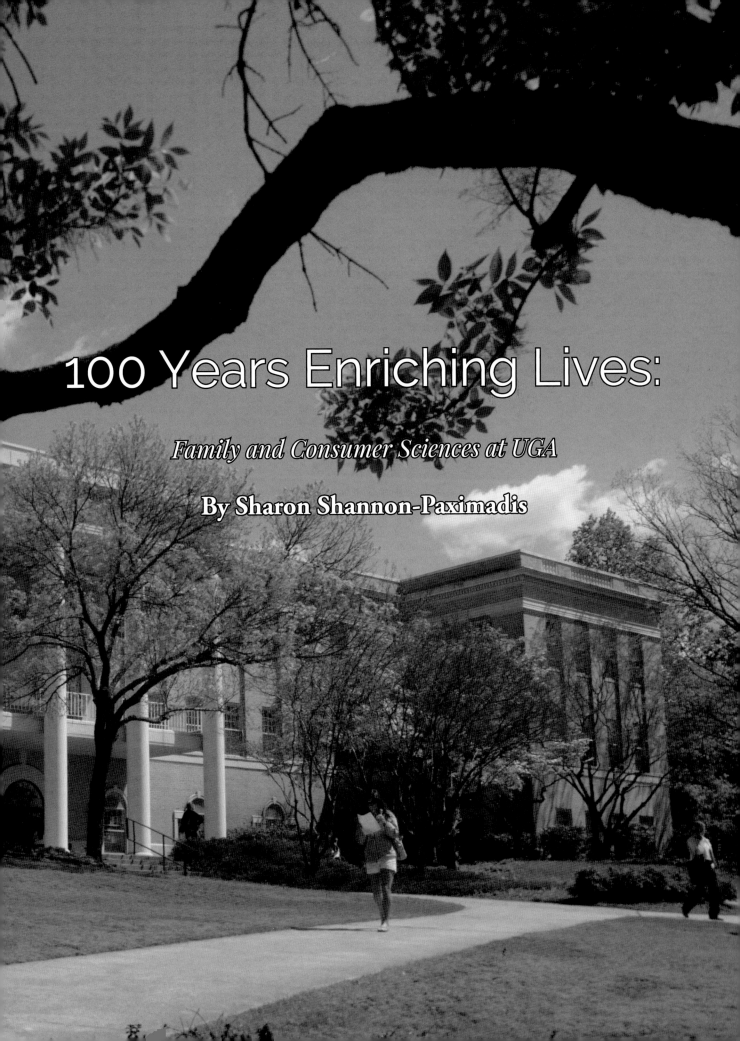

100 Years Enriching Lives:

Family and Consumer Sciences at UGA

By Sharon Shannon-Paximadis

The Donning Company Publishers

731 South Brunswick Street

Brookfield, MO 64628

Lex Cavanah, General Manager

Nathan Stufflebean, Production Supervisor

Philip Briscoe, Editor

Todd Erwin, Graphic Designer

Katie Gardner, Marketing and Project Coordinator

Susan Adams, Project Research Coordinator

Lynn Walton, Project Director

Library of Congress Cataloging-in-Publication Data

On file with the Library of Congress

ISBN: 978-0-8203-5451-4

Printed in the United States of America at Walsworth

Dedication

To the women and men who led the way, enriching the lives of individuals, families, and communities across Georgia through the development and growth of the field of home economics at the University of Georgia . . .

To those who continue to shape the future of Family and Consumer Sciences at UGA today . . .

And to future generations of UGA FACS students, faculty, and staff, as you carry on the tradition of enriching lives through teaching, research, and public service into the next 100 years.

FACS 100

Centennial Celebration Sponsors

Centennial Champion
Elwood & Goetz Wealth Advisory Group
Georgia United Credit Union
Lanier Apparel/Oxford Industries

Friend of the Gala
Jenna and Clanton Black
Wayne and Linda Kirk Fox
Camille and Paul Kesler
Kathy and Danny Palmer
Matrix Residential
Edie and Lamar Smith
Lynda Cowart Talmadge
The Quadrillion

Centennial Host
Geoffrey Warren Bell
Megan and Michael Crook
Sandra Whaley Derrick and Sid Derrick
Theresa Lynn Glasheen
Patricia Dabbs Hackney and Howard Hackney
Jennifer and Greg Holcomb
Debbie and Lowell Murray
Claudia and John Noell
Cara and Andre Simmons
Jessica Tripp
Bonnie Stephens Petersen and Clark E. Petersen
Marilyn L. Poole
Deborah Burgess Wise and Asha Wise

Centennial Enthusiast
Lindsey Derrick
Heidi Harriman Ewen
Parks McLeod, Jr.

Foreword

On behalf of the University of Georgia, I am delighted to congratulate the College of Family and Consumer Sciences on reaching its centennial. This significant milestone provides a special opportunity for the University community to celebrate the college's past 100 years of enriching lives—the lives of students, faculty, staff, and the citizens of this state and beyond, who benefit from its outstanding academic and outreach programs.

As we mark this anniversary, it is important to remember the role the college played in helping women achieve higher education at this University. The college's forebearer, the Division of Home Economics, was the academic home to Mary Ethel Creswell, who in 1919 became the first woman to receive an undergraduate degree from UGA and went on to serve as the college's first dean. Over the decades that followed, the college has expanded to include four departments, one institute, and 16 research laboratories and centers.

Today, powered by dedicated and talented faculty members, the college is at the forefront of advancing UGA's commitment to improving the world around us. Academic programs—ranging from human development and dietetics to financial planning and fashion merchandising—prepare students for leadership roles in a variety of careers. Critical research conducted by faculty members is helping to combat obesity, prevent disease, respond to economic challenges, and address many other pressing issues facing our state and nation in the 21st century.

As the pages that follow make clear, for 100 years the College of Family and Consumer Sciences has provided leadership through its outstanding teaching, research, and public service. As we look to the next 100 years, I am certain that the college will continue on its course to enhance lives and communities for generations to come.

Jere W. Morehead
President, University of Georgia

Preface

On the happy occasion of our centennial in 2018, I am deeply proud of our past.

The people and the stories contained in these pages inspire me, as they will you. Those who went before us at the University of Georgia were agents of change in the times they were born into, no matter the circumstance.

Our history began a century ago, when World War I—along with the desperate need for technically trained female teachers and home demonstration agents—ended the resistance to women enrolling at UGA. The women who went before us were driven to learn and understand more, to do more with their education, and to contribute more to improving the lives of others.

This book is designed to show how, through the history of home economics at UGA (now family and consumer sciences), our programs have responded during periods of change and the conditions at the time in our country, and indeed, in the world.

We hope you enjoy reading through the timeline and the personal vignettes of noteworthy alumni, faculty, and college leadership. One hundred years is certainly a long time. There are so many people who have played an important role in the development and advancement of our college. No doubt we've overlooked or, quite frankly, were unaware of a key figure or an event or two, no matter how thorough the search of the archives. Please use this opportunity to reach out to the college to tell us who else should be part of this ongoing celebration. After all, we are all participating in history and we can all contribute to the collective reflection on 100 years!

While proud of our past, I'm also just as excited for our future. Our current faculty, students, and alumni are building on the fine tradition of the trailblazers who came before us, pursuing exciting research and innovative outreach projects that will positively impact Georgians for years to come.

Today, our college boasts strong, accredited, and nationally recognized degree programs. Our faculty and staff continue to be student-centered as we strive to progressively prepare the next generation of professionals, the women and men who graduate from our college, to address the challenges facing the world.

When celebrating any birthday, it's healthy and informative to look back, as these pages will demonstrate. However, we must also remember to "blow out the candles and make a wish." Our wish is for a brighter and better future.

What is my wish for the future? My wish is for many new achievements to be added to our impressive continuum of innovation, and I eagerly await the next of several "firsts" still to come as we boldly set out into our second century.

Please remain engaged and be an active part of the history we are making, today and every day!

Linda Kirk Fox
Dean, College of Family and Consumer Sciences

Acknowledgements

Chronicling the 100-year history of the College of Family and Consumer Sciences at UGA, in just a few short months, would have been a daunting task were it not for the dedicated team who gave of their time, energy, and expertise to bring this ambitious project to completion. Please know how much your contributions are appreciated.

UGA College of Family and Consumer Sciences

Don Bower, Professor Emeritus and Extension Specialist

Linda Kirk Fox, Dean

Patti Hunt-Hurst, Associate Dean for Academic Programs

Sharon Y. Nickols, Dean and Professor Emerita

Cal Powell, Director of Communications

Monica Sklar, Historic Clothing and Textile Collection

Anne Sweaney, Josiah Meigs Distinguished Teaching Professor and Professor Emerita

UGA Terry College of Business

Katrina Bowers, Senior Director of Development and Alumni Relations

UGA College of Agricultural and Environmental Sciences

Josh Paine, Marketing Specialist

Student Contributors

Taylor Coleman
Vivian Hubby
Hannah Norton

Alumni

Debbie Phillips, President, The Quadrillion
John McNamara, Emeritus Professor of Animal Sciences, Washington State University

University Libraries – Hargrett Rare Book and Manuscript Library

Katherine Stein, Director

Mary Linneman, Digital Imaging Associate

And all the Reading Room Monitors

University Libraries – Special Collections, Oral History Program

Christian Lopez, Head, Oral History Program
Iva Dimitrova, Oral History Coordinator

University Libraries – Richard B. Russell Library for Political Science and Studies

Sheryl Vogt, Director

University of Georgia Press

Lisa Bayer, Director
Melissa Buchanan, Assistant EDP Manager

Bulldog Print + Design

Ronda Wynveen, Graphic Technician

Georgia Museum of Art

Hillary Brown, Director of Communications

Although the history of Family and Consumer Sciences at the University of Georgia begins in 1918, the contributions made by trailblazers such as Catharine Beecher, Maria Parloa, Nellie Sawyer Kedzie, Marion Talbot, and Ellen H. Swallow Richards in the late 1800s cannot be overstated. They, like many others, worked tirelessly to bring the principles of domestic science to the general public. Richards, in particular, was instrumental in the development, and promotion, of scientific theories and techniques applied to the home and family.

With the passing of the Morrill Act in 1862 (which provided funding for land-grant colleges in each state), higher education was expanded beyond the more traditional professions of medicine, law, and the ministry to include research and instruction in subjects such as agronomy, horticulture, animal science, nutrition, textiles and clothing, and sanitary education. The US Department of Agriculture was created by President Abraham Lincoln that same year. Shortly thereafter, in 1887, the Hatch Act would provide for the formation of State Agricultural Experiment Stations. Their purpose was to develop and improve agricultural practices and the rural home—and the welfare of consumers—through research and education.

The Second Morrill Act, passed into law in 1890, provided funding for the establishment of public, land-grant colleges and universities, located predominantly in southern and border states, to provide education for African Americans in agriculture, the mechanical arts, and domestic science. Reflecting on the passage of this legislation and its importance to the home economics movement, Carrie A. Lyford writes in *A Study of Home Economics Education in Teaching Institutions for Negroes*, "The extension demonstrations by the Negro agents are unquestionably among the most important lessons in homemaking carried on in the South today."

Beginning in 1899, Ellen Swallow Richards and her contemporaries organized a series of annual meetings, known as the Lake Placid Conferences. During the first conference, it was agreed that the term "home economics" would be used to describe all aspects of home management. In 1908, conference attendees formed the American Home Economics Association, officially establishing home economics as a profession. Their efforts would increase federal and state funding of home economics research and education.

> *Many of the people that were involved in home economics were also involved in some of the Progressive Era political movements, and some of the individuals involved in the political movements were very supportive of home economics, because they saw it as a way to improve living conditions, and for people to better themselves and ultimately, then, to better society.*

—Dr. Sharon Y. Nickols,
Dean and Professor Emerita

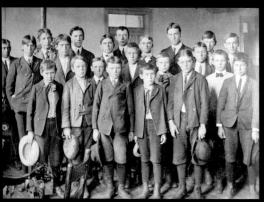

In 1904, the first "Corn Club" was formed in Georgia, followed by similar after-school agricultural clubs throughout the state. Gardening and canning clubs soon followed. A forerunner of the 4-H clubs, the goal was to help acquaint rural youngsters with new agricultural techniques and processes. According to the national 4-H website, "The idea of practical and 'hands-on' learning came from the desire to connect public school education to country life. Building community clubs to help solve agricultural challenges was a first step toward youth learning more about the industries in their community."

The Smith-Lever Act of 1914, co-sponsored by Senator Hoke Smith (D-Ga.) and Representative Asbury Lever (D-S.C.), created a national Cooperative Extension Service as part of the US Department of Agriculture. The organization provided outreach programs through land-grant universities to educate rural Americans about advances in agricultural practices and technology, with the initial goal of stabilizing the nation's food production. Home Demonstration Clubs were started to provide rural families with home improvement and labor-saving techniques. At the same time, 4-H clubs were being organized across the country to promote the building of leadership skills and community service among the nation's youth.

Today, more than six million young people participate in 4-H programs throughout the United States. In Georgia, UGA Extension agents work in county offices across the state, providing a link between the University and the public. The organization is a county, state, and federally funded unit supported by specialists in the College of Agricultural and Environmental Sciences and the College of Family and Consumer Sciences.

"I think one of the strengths of the Extension system is the fact that it is bottom up. We develop needs-based programming and a needs-assessment process, that instead of someone in Athens or a state capital or D.C. deciding what the priorities need to be, we really take seriously our responsibility to the public to understand what their needs are in terms of the context of what we can provide."

—Dr. Don Bower, Professor Emeritus and Extension Specialist

Within the first decades of the 20th century, the transition from a predominantly rural, agricultural-based economy to one more focused on manufacturing in an urban arena was underway across the United States. Cities such as New York, Philadelphia, New Orleans, and San Francisco experienced significant growth during these years. In Georgia, according to the US Census Bureau, the urban population grew by more than 25 percent between 1910 and 1920, while the state's rural population grew by less than 5 percent. Americans were on the move, literally, from the farmland to the factories. By 1918, automobile manufacturers were selling more than 1.6 million cars per year; vehicle registrations in the United States surpassed 6.1 million.

The period was not without unrest however. Issues surrounding urbanization, industrialization, immigration, and government corruption necessitated the implementation of many economic, political, and social reforms. America's entry into World War I, in 1917, added to the social unrest, as millions of women entered the workforce and raised their collective voices to demand access to higher education and the right to vote. The advancement of the domestic sciences became a top priority for many advocates of the feminist movement. However, southern states—including Georgia—were slow to address these issues. In her book *The Politics of Education in the New South: Women and Reform in Georgia 1890–1930,* author Rebecca S. Montgomery writes, "The reasons were at least partially rooted in the antebellum social structure. Much of the opposition was similar to that faced by professionals throughout the nation—critics charged that homemaking was a personal matter learned in the home and that formal instruction was either a frivolous waste of time or an attempt to turn rural, working-class girls into servants."

CHAPTER 1

From Opposition to Expansion

1918–1928

By 1918, champions of the effort to allow undergraduate women admission to the University of Georgia—and to create a Division of Home Economics—were still encountering significant opposition. An editorial published in the Lawrenceville (Georgia) News-Herald on January 28, 1918, proclaimed, "Some of the leading women behind this propaganda have openly admitted that one of their purposes is to . . . make timid and bashful girls more self reliant, self assertive and independent, which means, in its last analysis, the destruction of that modesty and real refinement that make them so attractive to men."

Despite opposition on a number of fronts, expansion of the development of, and education in, home economics during the early 20th century could not be held at bay. The demand for educated and experienced home economics professionals continued to rise as the effects of World War I were felt nationwide. The shortage of food products and other basic resources made knowledge of nutrition, food preservation, and clothing and textiles even more valuable. The home economics movement was destined to bring more science to both rural and urban households while providing women with a path to higher education and leadership roles in public education, academia, government, and industry.

TIMELINE

1917 – The Smith-Hughes Act, or the National Vocational Education Act, is signed into law. The legislation provides funds for vocational teaching of agriculture, trades and industries, commerce, and home economics in high schools. Senator Hoke Smith and Representative D. M. Hughes, both of Georgia, champion the effort. Eighty-eight home demonstration agents were employed in 85 Georgia counties.

1917 – The American Dietetic Association is founded to aid consumers in food conservation and to improve general health and nutrition during World War I. The association, now known as the Academy of Nutrition and Dietetics, currently represents more than 100,000 food and nutrition professionals.

1918 – The First World War ends.

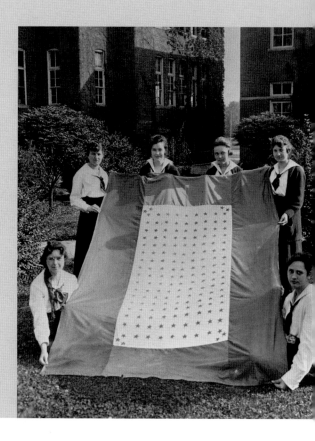

1918 – The Division of Home Economics is founded at UGA. The first degree course for women, a bachelor of science in the College of Agriculture, is approved. State College of Agriculture president Andrew Soule names Mary Ethel Creswell (1879–1960) director of the newly created division. Twelve students are enrolled.

"Talk about a touchy enterprise. Women had proved themselves in many fields during the First World War and the trades and professions were being grudgingly opened to them. But here we were preparing to invade territory that has been exclusively male since its remote beginnings. Young women of today, with their easy acceptance of many privileges another generation had to fight and brave ridicule to win, simply cannot understand that not only the men students, but many mature men of influence, were absolutely rigid and rockbound in their opposition toward swinging the University gates wide to women. Wide, did I say? We were to be the opening wedge!"

—Mary Ethel Creswell, 1951

FACS FAST FACT

Courses Offered for the 1918–1919 School Year:

- Foods and Cookery Group
- Textiles and Clothing
- Home Administration
- Education Group
- Winter Short Courses

Students must also complete six credit hours of chemistry, botany, zoology, physiology, and physics; six credit hours from horticulture, agronomy, poultry, dairy, and plant pathology; six credits from history, education, English, economics, and sociology; and six credit hours of general electives.

1918 – UGA Dairy Division provides food laboratory space and a cafeteria in Conner Hall. Space in the former home of Georgia governor Wilson Lumpkin, now Lumpkin Hall, is designated for rest and study. "The Student Cottage," located near the Cedar Street entrance to campus, serves as the residence for the women students. Male students, wielding the "Co-ed Axe," kept the residence stacked with chopped kindling to fuel the many fireplaces in the home.

Martha "Atalanta" Lumpkin's Spinning Wheel, 1918

Known as Aunt Maddie to her family, the legacy of Martha "Atalanta" Lumpkin, the daughter of Governor Wilson Lumpkin, lives on to this day. According to several accounts, the city of Atlanta was originally named Marthaville in her honor. It was then changed in 1845 to Atlanta as an abbreviated version of her nickname Atalanta, known in Greek mythology as an athletic and swift huntress. In the spring of 1918, Aunt Maddie's nephew, UGA chancellor David Barrow, informs Home Economics director Mary Creswell that "we are moving some of my Aunt Mattie's furniture [from Lumpkin Hall] to make way for Home Economics. Would you like to have Aunt Mattie's spinning wheel?" Creswell said yes, making it the first gift to the new Division of Home Economics.

1918 – The flu pandemic of 1918 sickens nearly 25 percent of the US population, ultimately claiming nearly 675,000 lives. Home demonstration kitchens are frequently converted into production kitchens where hearty soups and other foods can be prepared and distributed to families in need.

1918 – Construction of the Women's Building (later named Soule Hall) begins. A 400-pound bell, crafted in 1915 by the McShane Foundry Company of Baltimore, Maryland, is believed to have served as a dinner bell for the female residents. The bell, which came to be known as the "Jennie Bell" in honor of Soule Hall housemother Jennie Belle Myers, continues to enjoy a long and storied history with the university.

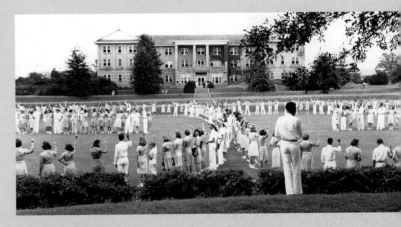

COMMEMORATING
THE ADMISSION OF WOMEN TO
THE STATE COLLEGE OF AGRICULTURE
UNIVERSITY OF GEORGIA
SEPT. 1918

1919 – In his Annual Report, College of Agriculture president Andrew Soule calls for the expansion of the Division of Home Economics to a four-year course to provide training for extension work, high school teaching, institutional management, and the agricultural industry, as well as technical and research work for federal and state agencies.

1919 – Mary Creswell, director of Home Economics, becomes the first woman to receive an earned bachelor's degree at the University of Georgia.

1919 – Mrs. Lenna Gertrude Judd makes the first monetary gift to the Division of Home Economics, $3,000, in memory of her late husband, to equip the Morton Ellis Judd Nutrition Laboratory in Soule Hall. The laboratory would be moved to Dawson Hall in 1932, and then again in 1971 to the Dawson Hall Annex (Speirs Hall).

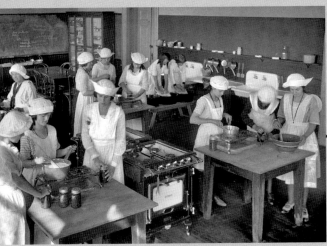

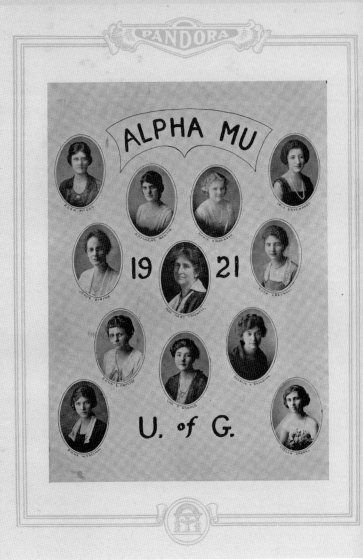

1920 – Soule Hall, named for College of Agriculture president Andrew Soule, opens. The first dormitory for women includes 37 bedrooms, a gymnasium, a laboratory, classrooms, a swimming pool, and a lounge.

1920 – Alpha Mu, an honorary home economics society is established with 12 members.

1920 – Passage of the 19th Amendment of the US Constitution gives women the right to vote.

1920 – The "First 12" UGA home economics students graduate with BSHE degrees.

1921 – Freshmen and sophomore women are admitted to the UGA home economics program.

1922 – The Enabling Act is passed by the Georgia legislature allowing county authorities to use tax money to support county Extension Service agents, home demonstration agents, and vocational teachers in both agricultural and home economics education.

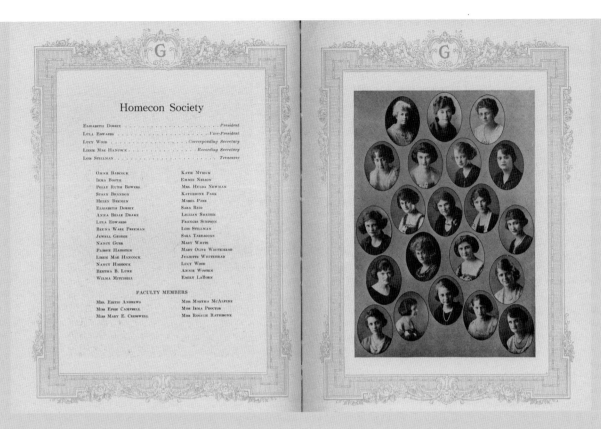

1922 – The Homecon Club is established for all UGA home economics students. The club has 32 student members and six faculty advisors.

1923 – Frigidaire introduces the first self-contained refrigerator. The suggested retail price is $285.

1923 – The US Bureau of Home Economics is established to generate standardized consumer information. Dr. Louise Stanley, PhD, of the University of Missouri, is appointed director. Research studies on nutrition, the best ways to prepare food, to clean, to sew, and to purchase clothing are conducted by the bureau.

"The welfare of any group is based on the combination of efficient production and wise consumption. There has been a tendency to study and develop the former to the neglect of the latter. The closer the adjustment between production and home demands the greater the economy to all, especially if the home demands are so directed as to promote health, efficiency, and well-being of the individuals."

—Louise Stanley, PhD
Report of the Chief of the Bureau of Home Economics, 1925

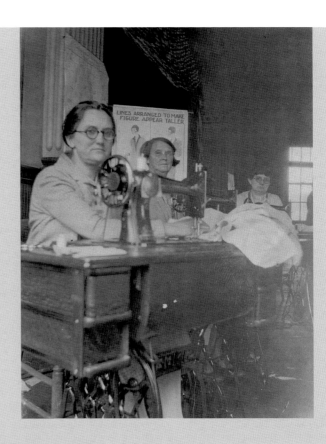

1923 – The master of science degree in home economics is established with a major in foods and nutrition. Three students are enrolled. The following year, a graduate minor in costume design is added.

1924 – The name "rayon" is created to describe regenerated cellulose fiber, the silk-like decorative fabric used for clothing. Home economists, with extensive training in textiles, fabrics, and clothing, work to develop standards and guide consumer purchasing.

1925 – Passage of the Purnell Act provides funds to land-grant colleges for rural home management studies. The study of dietary habits and research into the vitamin and mineral content of foods prevalent in rural Georgia are among the early subjects studied. Research is conducted in cooperation with the Georgia Experiment Station under the guidance of Katherine Newton, associate professor of foods and nutrition, and UGA graduate Lucile Turner.

1926 – Mary Ella Lunday joins the home economics staff as physical director. Sports-related activities such as archery, basketball, baseball, rifle, tennis, swimming, and dance are available.

1926 – The first nursery school for children, ages two to five years old, is established, providing students with the opportunity to observe and study preschool children. The Laura Spelman Rockefeller Foundation grants $18,000 for research in child development and for field work in parent education.

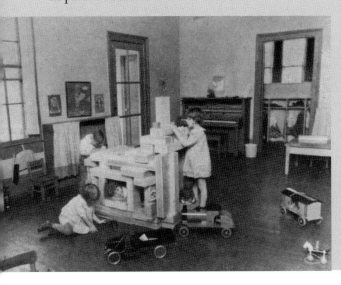

1926 – Home economics students, studying institutional management and catering, prepare and coordinate the "Football Players Banquet," which serves players and coaches each fall.

1927 – A new Art Department is established within the College of Agriculture and added to the Division of Home Economics. Andrew Soule, president of the College of Agriculture, stated that the program would include instruction in "drawing, painting, clay work, designing, and art work." The Child Development and Parent Education Department is also added that year.

1928 – A Household Equipment Laboratory, built in cooperation with Georgia Power Company and other commercial enterprises, furthers the study of home electrical equipment.

FACS FAST FACT

Home Economics Enrollment:

1918 – 12 students

1922 – 91 students

1925 – 105 students

1928 – 143 students

Personal Journey – Mary Ethel Creswell

Much has been written about Mary Creswell—her background, her work with the Girls Clubs, the USDA Extension Service, and Home Demonstration Clubs, as well as her unwavering commitment to higher education for women, and of her long and distinguished career at the University of Georgia.

Lending some insight into her personal dedication is an excerpt from a letter she wrote to her mother on January 21, 1918. In it, she writes, "There is a long story to tell you about the announcement of the new Home Economics Dept. for women in the College. The thing in brief of importance to me is that I am coming back to take charge of all the women's work and develop the new Department which will mean the opening of the university to women. There is every reason to believe that it will be a beautiful opportunity to make a fine development for the college and you know I am more happy over it than over anything which has happened to me in a long time. I will have a salary of $2500 and enough workers to do the work well."

Her personal achievements and contributions to home economics at UGA, and the accolades afforded her throughout her life, have been well documented—from her appointment as the first director of Home Economics by State College of Agriculture president Andrew Soule in 1918, to serving as the first president of the Georgia Home Economics Association in 1920, to being named the first dean of the UGA School of Home Economics in 1933.

Mary Creswell retired as dean in 1945, though she continued to teach classes until 1949. That same year, she was the first female recipient of the Alumni Award for outstanding service to the university. She served as president of the UGA chapter of the Phi Kappa Phi from 1949 to 1950. She died at home in Athens on August 7, 1960.

The newly constructed Creswell Dormitory was named in her honor in 1963. In 1980, Creswell was the first inductee into the College of Home Economics Honor Hall of Recognition.

In addition to building the School of Home Economics at UGA, Creswell had a dream to one day build her own home. In their article "The Opening Wedge: Mary E. Creswell, Home Economics, and the University of Georgia," authors Sharon Y. Nickols and Gina Gould Peek write, "What about the house Creswell hoped to build? She did indeed have a home of her own, located on Milledge Circle in Athens. The house is there today, sheltered by a now-immense ginkgo tree planted by Creswell decades ago. Each fall, the tree is resplendent in its golden leaves. It is a fitting metaphor for the academic program Creswell nurtured over the years. The Division of Home Economics is now the College of Family and Consumer Sciences, a vital program branching out to offer students a multitude of academic options and serving the public through Extension and research."

CHAPTER 2

Black Tuesday and the New Deal

1929–1940

T he rapid economic growth, social change, and unprecedented speculative spending prominent during the 1920s came to an abrupt halt late in 1929. Fueled by margin sellers, short-selling, and concern over European markets, Wall Street lost the equivalent of $30 billion in value in just four days ($423.5 billion in 2017 dollars), ushering in the start of the greatest worldwide economic depression in history. Many Americans lost everything. Banks across the country closed, consumer confidence hit a record low, and unemployment skyrocketed to nearly 25 percent.

The Great Depression hit Georgia and other southern states particularly hard. Cotton prices had begun to drop with the arrival of foreign competition and the introduction of synthetic fabrics. Many land owners, who had relied heavily on cash-crop production (producing crops for sale rather than for personal food), were forced out by large farmers who had moved away from cotton production and

into soybeans, corn, and peanuts, as well as raising livestock. 4-H clubs and home demonstration agents across the state were challenged to adjust their programs and activities to meet the needs of a rapidly growing population of rural poor. Enrollment in the School of Home Economics remained relatively stable until 1940, when incoming students numbered more than 400.

It would take the election of President Franklin Delano Roosevelt in 1932 to begin a new era of economic growth and recovery. The passing of unprecedented legislation and implementation of Roosevelt's "New Deal" would stabilize the banking industry, stimulate manufacturing and agricultural production, and put Americans back to work. The Works Progress Administration (WPA), the Civilian Conservation Corp (CCC), the Federal Emergency Relief Administration, the Agricultural Adjustment Administration (AAA), and the Soil Conservation Service were among the initiatives created. Many of these programs required experienced workers in the field of home economics. A number of UGA School of Home Economics faculty members went to work with the Farm Security Administration, established in 1935.

However, the implementation of many of Roosevelt's initiatives was stalled in Georgia by the governor at the time, Eugene Talmadge. His election platform in 1932, which promised tax cuts, the reduction of state services, and continued support for segregation, did not align well with the new federal agenda. Talmadge felt that efforts by the Roosevelt administration amounted to excessive intrusion, which he characterized as a "communistic experiment." It would be 1936 before the newly elected governor, E. D. Rivers, would bring many of the much-needed reforms to the state.

TIMELINE

1929 – The University of Georgia hosts its first home football game in the new, $360,000 Sanford Stadium. The UGA Bulldogs defeat the Yale Bulldogs 15-0. UGA would go on to finish the season with a 6-4 record.

1929 – The home equipment laboratory, established in 1928, is moved to larger rooms on the second floor of Barrow Hall. Visitors from 24 states come to observe the modern equipment donated by local manufacturers and utility companies.

1930 – The state of Georgia experiences its worst drought in recorded history, leading home demonstration teams to focus on food production, nutrition, and food preservation. The drought would last well into the following year.

In the old days of Extension in the 1920s and '30s, it was not uncommon for an agent, what was called then a home demonstration agent, even before cars, to ride a mule out to do a home visit and spend the night in that home so that she could ride to the next homestead the next day and, at some point, ride her mule or horse back to the office. We talk in Extension about having a missionary zeal. I think that's true to a great extent.

—Dr. Don Bower, Professor Emeritus and Extension Specialist

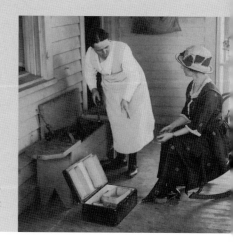

FACS FAST FACT

In 1931, the Division of Home Economics of the Georgia College of Agriculture and the Department of Home Economics of the State Normal School (Georgia State Teachers' College, Athens) are transferred to the Board of Regents of the University System. The merger creates the University of Georgia School of Home Economics.

1931 – A special regional short course, titled "Behavior Problems in Children," is held by the UGA School of Home Economics. The course, funded by the Laura Spelman Rockefeller Foundation, draws participants from Georgia, Florida, Alabama, and Cuba.

1931 – The Georgia General Assembly authorizes the reorganization of higher education in Georgia to a University System to be administered by a board of regents.

1931 – The price of raw cotton, one of Georgia's core agricultural products, drops to an unprecedented low of 5.66 cents/pound from its high of 28.88 cents/pound in 1918.

FACS FAST FACT

Student Expenses in 1932:
- Total annual entrance fees, room, board, and laundry: $495.50
- Meals served in Dawson Hall: $70/quarter
- $8,193.81 in 2017 dollars!

1932 – With a gift of $120,000 from the estate of Dr. William Terrell Dawson, a new three-story brick building for the School of Home Economics is built and named Dawson Hall. Given the economic challenges of the day, construction of the building was expedited so funding would not be redirected to other projects. The new Dawson Hall included four food labs, a cafeteria, and a clothing and textiles laboratory, as well as three studios for fine and applied arts.

Another campus landmark, Terrell Hall, was named for Dawson's grandfather and namesake, D. William Terrell. It was built in 1903 to replace Science Hall. Today, Terrell Hall houses the University Admissions Office and the Graduate School.

1932 – The first home management house is built to provide students with hands-on, real-life research and study opportunities. Funding is provided by the Works Progress Administration (WPA).

1933 – A four-day closure of all banks is ordered to allow Congress to pass legislation that would address consumers' growing unrest.

1933 – Enrollment in the School of Home Economics more than doubles to 299 students.

Home Economics Club

An organization to develop leadership and to create a better spirit of fellowship and an interest in State, National, and International Home Economics work.

OFFICERS

RUTH MAYNARD	President
HELEN SMITH	Vice-President
CAROLYN LATIMER	Secretary
RUTH DICKSON	Treasurer

IN PICTURE FROM TOP - LEFT TO RIGHT - *First row:* Maynard, Smith, Latimer, Dickson, Dillard, Ellington. *Second row:* Carlton, Hatcher, Fleming, Pennington, Colquitt, Hale. *Third row:* Clarkson, Calloway, Pool, Carlton, Jackson.

MEMBERS

Jo Lynn Aderhold	Willouese Fambro	Bess Kelly	Idelle Pennington
Katherine Baker	Rosalyn Fargason	Laura Kirkland	Marion Pennington
Grace Barrett	Clora Fitzgerald	Carolyn Latimer	Linnell Perkins
Kathryn Bass	Lois Flanagan	Lola Bell Livesey	Lois Petit
Christine Brim	Bessie Neal Fleming	Elizabeth Livesey	Bernice Pool
Christine Calloway	Frances George	Ella Levie	Marguerite Pool
Daisy Campbell	Hallie Griffeth	Odelle Martin	Myrtle Slade
Annie Jim Carlton	Sara Allen Hale	Myrtie Lee McGoogan	Helen Smith
Cornelia Carlton	Lauree Hatcher	Cammie Maynard	Sara Souther
Amanda Clarkson	Kathleen Hobgood	Ruth Maynard	Elizabeth Stewart
Mattie Kate Colquitt	Montine Jackson	Mae Monroe	Margaret Webb
Ruth Dickson	Elizabeth Johnson	Louise Morgan	Emelyn Westbrook
Lois Dillard	Ollie Johnson	Wilma Nix	Evelyn Williams
Louise Ellington	Emmie Lee Jordan	Marian Payne	Sara Frances Yarbrough
			Mary Young

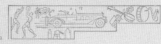

. 269 .

1933 – Mary Creswell is named the first dean of the UGA School of Home Economics.

FACS FAST FACT

Career Choices of BSHE Degree Recipients in 1933:

• Teaching	21
• Extension Agents	10
• Graduate Students	6
• Homemakers	5
• Commercial Positions	4
• Research	1
• Miscellaneous	5
Total	52

1934 – The second of four home management houses, also funded by the Works Progress Administration (WPA), is built on campus.

1934 – Financial challenges force the university to cease funding of the nursery school. Funding is obtained through the Works Progress Administration (WPA).

1935 – Congress passes the Social Security Act, providing Americans—for the first time—with unemployment, disability, and pensions for old age.

1935 – The National Labor Relations Act is passed allowing for the unionization of Georgia's textile mills and factories. Minimum wages, working conditions, and working hours for industrial workers were also clearly defined. Child labor was eliminated and the school year was expanded to seven months. New schools were constructed, and textbooks were provided to students free of charge. The Rural Electrification Administration helped form electric cooperatives for the delivery of electricity to rural residents, and the Agricultural Adjustment Act gave farmers subsidies to limit overproduction of certain crops and drive up market prices.

1936 – The Chi chapter of Phi Upsilon Omicron, the Home Economics National Honor Society, is installed, replacing Alpha Mu. The new chapter has 35 members including 12 active, and numerous eligible alumni and honorary members.

According to their website, the purpose of Phi Upsilon Omicron continues to be to: "1. Recognize and promote academic excellence; 2. Develop qualities of leadership by providing opportunities for service; and 3. Encourage lifelong learning and commitment to advance family and consumer sciences and related fields." Today, the national organization has over 97,000 members.

Left to right: University System chancellor Steadman V. Sanford, Georgia governor Eurith D. Rivers, and President Franklin Delano Roosevelt

1937 – Margaret McPhaul is named director of the Nursery School. Funding responsibility for the facility moves to the School of Home Economics.

1938 – President Franklin Delano Roosevelt delivers the commencement address to the 1938 UGA graduating class and receives an honorary law degree. To accommodate the president's busy schedule, the commencement ceremony is moved up three weeks.

1939 – Two additional home management houses and a Child Development Lab are constructed with funding from the Works Progress Administration (WPA) program.

1940 – Snelling Dining Hall opens, resulting in the closure of the cafeteria in Dawson Hall. Still in operation today, Snelling Dining Hall offers food service to its more than 8,000 meal plan participants.

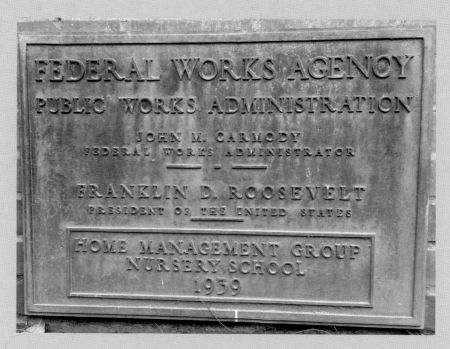

1940 – The Nursery School reopens in a new building built with Works Progress Administration (WPA) funds. The facility contains many of the latest features and serves as both a demonstration lab and teaching center.

1940 – A research project to determine the effects of diet deficiencies in humans is conducted by 48 junior and senior home economics students using laboratory rats. The test animals are fed a variety of diets based on an average food formula representing the various economic groups found in Georgia.

Each girl sees the results of proper and improper diets, and when she later becomes a teacher she is better fitted to instruct her pupils. Such work as we are doing is only a port(ion) of the University's program to let the students get practical as well as theoretical training in their studies.

—Katherine Newton, Associate Professor and Project Supervisor

1940 – The Georgia Nutrition Committee for National Defense is formed, bringing nutrition professionals together to address nutrition issues in Georgia. Lurline Collier is named first chair. The name of the organization is changed to the Georgia Nutrition Council (GNC) in 1950.

1940 – The first of many expansion projects is completed at Sanford Stadium with the installation of lights. The first night game has Georgia taking on Kentucky; the game ends in a 7-7 tie.

for Jackson County, a position she would hold until 1923 before entering the University of Georgia. Among her notable achievements during this time include starting a school lunch program where she prepared one hot dish daily on an old potbellied stove, and teaching sewing and cooking classes after school. She would also study at Purdue University and the University of Oklahoma.

After graduation, Collier returned to the state extension service in DeKalb County as a clothing specialist, and then became the state agent for Girl's Clubs. In 1933, she became the state home demonstration agent, the highest position for women in Georgia Extension Service at the time, and one she would hold until her retirement in 1953. She was the first Georgia Nutrition Committee chair, and served one term as president of the Georgia Home Economics Association. Collier also served on the Commission on the Status of Women, and the Executive Committee for Land Grant Colleges.

In a handwritten note Collier received shortly after her retirement, dear friend Mary Creswell writes,

a woman in the county. "I was made a Deputy to take care of legal papers while my father was away," Collier explained. According to the article, she never carried a gun while on duty or arrested anyone.

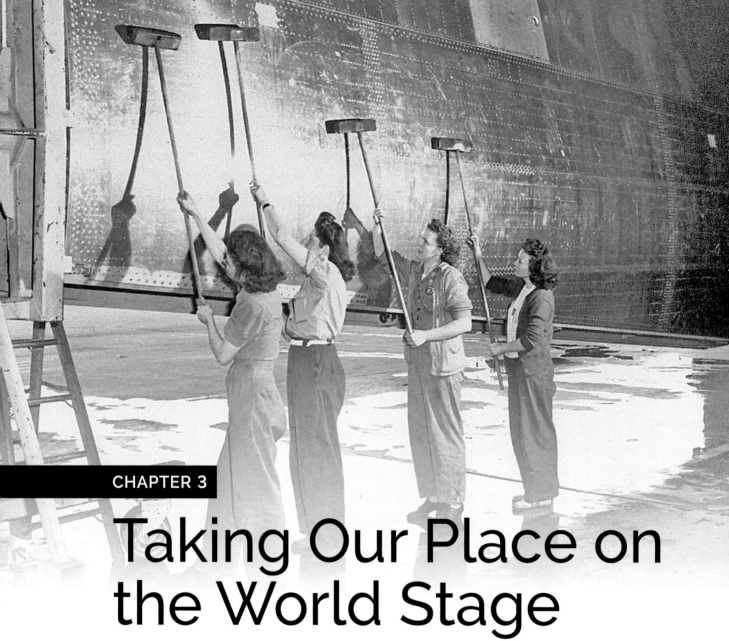

CHAPTER 3

Taking Our Place on the World Stage

1941–1945

The United States' entry into the Second World War in 1941 essentially brought the Great Depression to an end. In Georgia, the effect was profound. More than 320,000 Georgians served in the armed forces, and so many more worked in war-related industries. Defense contractors built plants throughout the state, bringing jobs and economic relief to the region. The B-29 bomber plant, located in Marietta, accounted for 28,000 jobs.

Life in rural areas of the state changed as well. The demand for agricultural products increased significantly as did market prices. Despite these economic improvements, however, many farm workers chose to vacate or sell their land to defense contractors in order to move to urban areas offering higher-paying jobs. For those who remained, the state extension service, and specifically, home demonstration agents, played an important role in bringing the latest techniques in food production and preservation, sewing and clothing repair, child development, and home management to residents throughout the state.

For the University of Georgia, and the School of Home Economics in particular, support of the war effort could be seen on many fronts. The US Navy occupied many areas of Dawson Hall beginning in 1942. Roughly 2,000 naval cadets completed pre-flight training while residing on campus. Soule, Rutherford, and Mary Lyndon residence halls were used for housing.

The political climate of the day would be parlayed onto the national stage as Governor Eugene Talmadge orchestrated the firing of numerous UGA professors and administrators for their support of a racially integrated demonstration school in Athens. Talmadge vowed to remove anyone who supported "communism or racial equality." The Southern Association of Colleges and Schools, citing "gross political interference," withdrew accreditation from all state-supported schools—including the University of Georgia—in 1941. Accreditation would be restored the following year under newly elected governor Ellis Arnall.

TIMELINE

1941 – In support of the war effort, an emphasis on conservation can be seen in the home economics course of study. Topics include the remodeling and repairing of clothing, using cotton, managing family budgets, and meal planning. Research topics include Fears of Young Children (including those related to war), Play Behavior of Young Children, and Eating and Sleeping Habits of Children.

1941 – Working with the Red Cross, students make wool blankets for British refugees.

1941 –The American Home Economics Association encourages all senior home economics students and university staff, as well as all other home economists including demonstration agents and institutional managers, to register for home defense. One hundred twenty-nine UGA home economics students register.

The National Defense Advisory Commission has seen how these home economists can be valuable. If called upon, they will strengthen their communities by seeing that people in homes get the proper food, clothing, and care.

—*Athens Banner-Herald*, December 1941

SUGAR ~ FLOUR ~ CEREAL ~ SPICE

• Store dried foods in tight containers to keep out moisture, insects, dust, and mice.

• Watch out for weevils in hot weather.

CANNED FOODS

• Food in glass should be kept in a cool, dark place. Light affects color, and vitamins.

• Store tinned foods in dry place to prevent rust.

FIGHT FOOD WASTE *in the home*   BUREAU OF HOME ECONOMICS U.S. DEPARTMENT OF AGRICULTURE   10

FACS FAST FACT

Career Choices of BSHE Alumni in 1941:

• Teaching	111
• Extension Agents	17
• Dietitians	21
• Graduate Students	10
• Homemakers	24
• Commercial Positions	15
• Farm Security Administration	22
• Government Work	7
• Miscellaneous	14
Total	241

1941 – The first Recommended Dietary Allowances (RDA) is published by the National Research Council to provide a framework for healthy nutrition. The RDA includes calories, protein, iron, calcium, and other vitamins.

1942 – Due to a shortage of nurses, the Red Cross provides a course in "Home Care of the Sick." Those completing the course receive certificates in "Home Nursing."

1942 – The first National 4-H Mobilization Week is organized by the Federal Extension Service. One goal is to recruit new members to replace those who have joined the military or gone to work for defense contractors. More than 650,000 members are recruited this year. Georgia 4-H membership grows to 110,000.

Your activities in producing, preserving, and preparing food; in making clothing; and your other practical experiences in farming and homemaking have prepared you for many tasks important in peacetime and indispensable in wartime. No other group of rural young people anywhere else in the world has so much worth defending, or is better prepared to help defend what it has.

—President Franklin D. Roosevelt
Announcement of the first 4-H Mobilization Week

1943 – The School of Home Economics establishes a preliminary plan for the education of returning servicemen and servicewomen. In addition to bachelor's and master's degree programs, the plan offers a one-year course of study for those interested in pursuing employment in restaurants, tea rooms, school lunch rooms, or in dressmaking. The plan also suggests a course in homemaking for the wives of returning servicemen.

1943 – The 25th year of the School of Home Economics at UGA. The Silver Anniversary celebration is delayed due to wartime emergencies.

1944 – Dean Mary Creswell is honored at the Silver Anniversary celebration for the School of Home Economics in June. A portrait of her, painted by well-known artist Wilford S. Conrow, is presented to the university. The chair used in the portrait still resides in Dawson Hall.

Creswell would retire as dean in 1945. She would continue to teach until 1949.

1944 – Jasper Guy Woodroof is named UGA Alumni Distinguished Professor of Food Science for his work in food preservation, including canning and freezing techniques. These processes are subsequently taught in home economics courses. Woodroof, associated with the Georgia Experiment Station from 1938 to 1967, is often referred to as the "father of food science." Among his wartime contributions is the process for preserving military rations.

FACS FAST FACT

Career Choices of BSHE Alumni in 1945:

- Teaching   285
- Extension Agents   52
- Dietitians   41
- Graduate Students   12
- Homemakers   52
- Commercial Positions   35
- Farm Security Administration   58
- Government Work   29
- Miscellaneous   18
        Total   582

FACS FAST FACT

Home Economics Enrollment:
    1941 – 424 students
    1943 – 285 students
    1945 – 276 students

1944 – The Historic Costume Collection is established as part of the school's Silver Anniversary. The mission is to document Georgia's history through the preservation of historic clothing and textiles. Students, faculty, and alumni are asked to contribute historical items. Today, the collection contains over 3,000 garments, accessories, and textiles, dating from the 1800s to present day, which provide examples of line, design, fabric, workmanship, and quality. It is used in instruction, research, and as a source for inspiration.

"We are saving a part of Georgia's history. What people wore is a part of history. It gives us a picture of what the conditions of the time were economically, politically, culturally and religiously."

—Dr. Patricia Hunt-Hurst
Dress and Fashion Historian, Professor and Associate
Dean for Academic Programs

1945 – World War II ends.

Personal Journey – Katherine Newton

As one of the original 12 members of Alpha Mu, the honorary UGA Home Economics Society founded in 1920, and a driving force behind the Homecon Club founded in 1922, Katherine "Kat" Newton left an indelible mark on the School of Home Economics, and specifically the study of food and nutrition.

Following her graduation in 1921, Newton's career in teaching and research spanned more than 40 years. However, perhaps it was for her commitment to home economics education and service—demonstrated through such organizations as the UGA Homecon Club, Phi Upsilon Omicron, the Georgia Home Economics Association, and the American Home Economics Association—that she will be long remembered.

In addition to her time as a member of the UGA faculty, Newton served as acting dean of the School of Home Economics following Mary Creswell's retirement in 1945. She returned to her position as professor in nutrition in 1946 and continued in this role until her retirement in 1965.

In celebration of her retirement, former students and colleagues were invited to share memories about their time with her at UGA, and to share thoughts on her numerous contributions.

"You were a marvelous teacher, firm but patient and understanding, and an enthusiastic leader for the two club groups. Part of any effectiveness I may have

achieved I attribute to you and 'the start' you gave me in Homecon."
—Janette McGarity Barber, State Department of Education

"One very special and meaningful word seems to epitomize your whole life and career to me. It is: dedicated. You are one of the reasons I am proud to say I am a home economist, so for myself and many others may I say, "WE OWE YOU SO MUCH."
— Gwen Brooks, Class of 1935

"Your untiring devotion to the virtues for which you stand, patience, honesty, humility and love, to name a few, has made you outstanding in the minds of many former students. Many of these girls were only (a) forming bud when they reached the University, but due to your heartfelt interest in the life they were going to lead, these buds grew into perfectly formed blossoms."
—Margie McIntyre, Clothing Specialist

"We wish for you great happiness in the years ahead and sincerely appreciate your dedicated services to this School which have contributed immeasurably to the growth of home economics and nutrition education in this State."
—Dr. Mary Speirs, Dean, College of Home Economics

Left to right: Katherine Newton, Arlevia Brisson, and Mary Barber

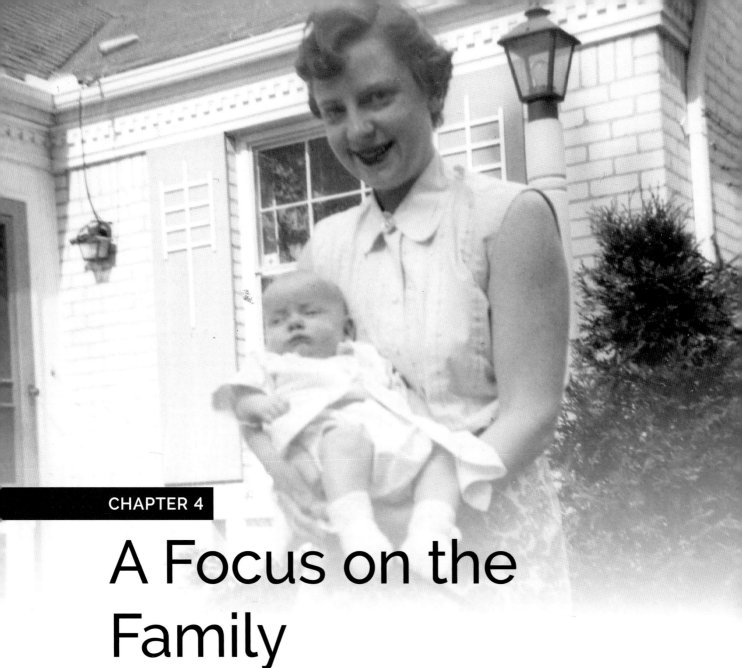

CHAPTER 4

A Focus on the Family

1946–1954

With the end of World War II, American servicemen and servicewomen returning from overseas found an overwhelming spirit of prosperity driven by a much-improved economy. Consumer goods were both bountiful and affordable. New financing options, including credit cards and charge accounts, served to increase consumer purchasing power. Societal changes placed a renewed emphasis on the family; women were encouraged to marry young, stay home, and raise children—and many did. According to the US Census Bureau, more than 33.5 million babies were born between 1946 and 1954. The US "Baby Boom" would continue until 1964.

In 1946, the United Nations established the Commission on the Status of Women, the first international effort to promote gender equality and empowerment. In an open letter addressed to "the women of the world," US delegate Eleanor Roosevelt wrote, "To this end, we call on the Governments of the world to encourage women everywhere to take a more active part in national and international affairs, and on women who are conscious of their opportunities to come forward and share in the work of peace and reconstruction as they did in war and resistance."

In Georgia, where 320,000 had served in the military during the war, the transition from a predominantly rural, agricultural society to one more urban and industrialized continued through this period. Policies such as the GI Bill, passed by Congress in 1944, made home ownership and higher education more accessible. Governor Ellis Arnall is credited with transitioning the image of the state from that of "Tobacco Road" to one more progressive and forward thinking. His reforms included balancing the state budget, returning accreditation to Georgia's universities, and establishing a teachers' retirement system.

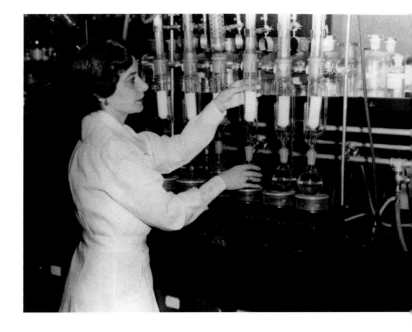

Support for public education, and research, led to changes on an academic level as well. The School of Home Economics would add courses designed to broaden core competencies and promote specialized accreditation, as evidenced by the creation of the Family Development Department in 1947. Courses in experimental foods would recognize a growing trend toward prepared and convenience foods, and the availability of new kitchen appliances. Numerous research studies would contribute to advancements in child development, nutrition, housing, and textile innovation.

TIMELINE

1946 – Dr. Pauline Park Wilson (Knapp) becomes dean of the School of Home Economics. Educated at the University of Kentucky and Columbia University, she serves until 1952. Knapp is credited with building the home economics research program, adding an infant laboratory to the nursery school, and increasing the number of majors offered by the school to nine. She also fostered relationships with the leaders of home economics programs throughout Georgia to strengthen and update course content and teaching practices.

1946 – Institutional management courses taught in university dining halls are designed to meet American Dietetic Association criteria.

1946 – The minimum wage is $0.40 per hour, and the average annual household income is $3,150. Staples such as bread cost $0.10 a loaf, milk is $0.70 a gallon, and a postage stamp costs just $0.03 cents. Accounting for inflation, the price of a gallon of milk translates into $9.29 today.

- -

1947 – The Family Development Department is established in the School of Home Economics. Dr. Dorothy Mummery joins the department to implement research programs and to help develop graduate courses. Among the many papers she publishes are "The Reliability and Validity of the Mummery Ascendance Score" in *Child Development*, vol. 21, no. 2, 1950, and "A Comparative Study of the Ascendant Behavior of Northern and Southern Nursery School Children" in *Child Development*, vol. 21, no. 3, 1950.

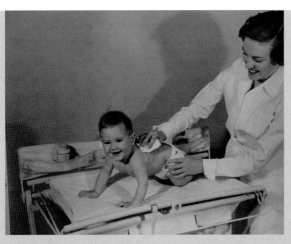

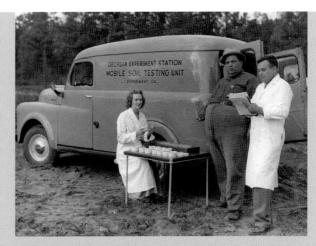

1947 – The infant laboratory is established as part of the UGA Nursery School. The lab provides students with the opportunity to study children under the age of two.

1947 – Dr. Maude Pye Hood is assigned to the Experiment Station for the Southern Regional Housing Research Project, a cooperative group of agricultural engineers and home economics serving eight southern states.

1947 – UGA chancellor Raymond Paty and the board of regents place the deans of forestry, home economics, and veterinary medicine on the administration staff of the College of Agriculture. The action is designed to further promote and expand extension work in each school.

1950 – The board of regents grants faculty status to Agricultural Experiment Station workers and the Georgia Agricultural Extension staff. This designation serves to build a closer relationship among teaching, research, and extension service workers. It also provides for better program coordination.

1950 – The number of research projects increases with a broader range of topics including regional housing, behavioral problems of children in nursery school, men's clothing preferences and related marketing factors, and how specific qualities of meats impact nutrition.

1950 – The fifth White House Conference on Children and Youth is held in Washington, DC. With more than 6,000 people in attendance, the conference is the first to address the emotional well-being of children. Organizers ask, "How can we develop in children the mental, emotional, and spiritual qualities essential to individual happiness and responsible citizenship?"

1950 – The Korean War begins when the Soviet-backed People's Republic of Korea invades the Republic of Korea to the south. In an article published July 6, 1950, in *The Red and Black*, students were asked to share their thoughts on the conflict. "Experts are calling the Far East affair everything from a minor diplomatic clash to the beginning of total war, but students prefer to remain optimistic about the outcome." Viewed as a war on communism, the three-year conflict would take nearly 40,000 American lives, 757 from Georgia.

1951 – Dean Knapp opens up classes to students not enrolled in the School of Home Economics and works to strengthen the relationship with the College of Education.

1951 – The Creswell Research Fund is established in honor of Mary Creswell. The fund provides faculty grants, graduate research funding, and funding for the acquisition of equipment used in research in the School of Home Economics.

1952 – Dean Knapp resigns to become president and director of the Merrill-Palmer School in Detroit, Michigan. The organization operates today as the Merrill-Palmer Skillman Institute and is part of Wayne State University. Dr. Maude Pye Hood is appointed acting dean, serving in this capacity until July 1954.

1952 – The US Navy agrees to pay the university $450,000 for Coordinate College, used since 1932 to house all freshmen and sophomore women enrolled in home economics. The property is converted into a training school for naval supply officers. In 2010, the property is returned to the university. It currently is part of the UGA Health Sciences Campus, formed in partnership with Augusta University.

1953 – Dr. Jessie J. Mize assumes the duties of chairman of research for the School of Home Economics. She would serve in this capacity for one year, allowing Acting Dean Hood to focus more fully on the Office of the Dean.

1953 – More than one million residential air conditioners are sold in the United States. Washing machines, electric dryers, stand mixers, toasters, and televisions are among the many items experiencing an increase in consumer demand. Home demonstration/extension agents and school teachers adapt their programs to incorporate these modern conveniences.

1953 – The number of master's degrees awarded to home economics students participating in the joint College of Education program reaches 28.

1953 – Myers Hall, named for home economics graduate and Soule Hall housemother Jennie Belle Myers, is completed. A 400-pound bell used to announce meals at Soule Hall is moved to the new residence hall. Nicknamed the "Jennie Bell," it would later be moved to Snelling Dining Hall.

1954 – The Foods and Nutrition Department faculty support legislation pertaining to the improvement of the nutritional value of bread flour, meat, and other important food items affecting the nutrition of low-income groups in Georgia.

1954 – Instructors from the Clothing and Textiles Department participate in extension work by serving as judges for county and state clothing competitions. They also work to build relationships with local retailers for coordinating fashion shows, demonstrations, and field trips.

1954 – Dr. Mary Speirs, chairman of research and head of Home Economics at the Georgia Experiment Station, and chair of the Division of Foods and Nutrition, is named dean of the School of Home Economics and coordinator of Home Economics Extension and Research. During her 17 years as dean, she would oversee the expansion of Dawson Hall as well as numerous research programs within the school.

1954 – A laboratory for the teaching of lunchroom management and catering for small groups is maintained in Dawson Hall. A home economics tea room, open to staff, students, and friends, is used for teaching food service management.

1954 – Dr. Maude Pye Hood accepts a three-year appointment in Pakistan as part of a joint venture between the Ford Foundation, Oklahoma State University, and the government of Pakistan to establish one of the first colleges of home economics in the country. According to their current website, the Ra'ana Liaquat Ali Khan Government College of Home Economics (RLAK CHE) is a top-ranking educational institute of Sindh, training highly skilled professionals for diverse careers such as educators, nutritionists, dietitians, designers, consultants, counselors, managers, and policy makers.

1954 – The elective courses available to home economics students are reviewed. Emphasis is placed on helping students prepare for a specific occupation through a major of general home economics. Joint programs are established with the College of Arts and Sciences and the Henry W. Grady School of Journalism.

FACS FAST FACT

Enrollment:

    1946 – 320 Students

    1949 – 293 Students

    1951 – 239 Students

    1954 – 219 Students

FACS FAST FACT

Top Professions for Home Economics Graduates in 1954:

- High School Home Economics Teachers
- Dietitians in hospitals, school lunch programs, and tea rooms
- Home Economists in business and government
- College Instructors

Personal Journey – Jessie Julia Mize

Jessie Julia Mize was born in Commerce, Georgia, in 1910. Following her graduation from Commerce High School, two years of study at the Georgia State Teacher's College, and two years of studying science at the University of Georgia, she received her bachelor of science degree in physics from UGA in 1930. She then earned a master of science degree in mathematics in 1931. With no advanced degrees available to women in either field of study, Mize next earned a bachelor of science degree in home economics in 1932. She would then go on to earn her PhD in family economics and household management from Cornell University in 1952.

Interior designers, kitchen planners, and remodelers—as well as anyone who spends time cooking—fully appreciate the role of the "kitchen triangle" in creating an efficient work environment. During her time at Cornell University pursuing a PhD, Mize participated in the research that led to the development of the Cornell kitchen, an innovative concept designed to improve functionality and efficiency through a working triangle that included the sink, the stove, and the refrigerator.

Experts in the fields of home economics, social psychology, engineering, and design were teamed together to look for ways to improve the one area of the home that was quickly becoming the center of family life—the kitchen. Research conducted by Mize and other home management specialists determined that excessive reaching, stooping, bending, and walking constituted a great deal of wasted energy. Sliding cabinet shelves, adjustable-height counters, wall-mounted ovens, and space-saving refrigerators were among the many innovations the research informed.

According to a promotional film produced by the Reynolds Metal Company in 1955, "If kitchen research is to be of ultimate benefit to the consumer, it must be of form and substance."

Upon her return to UGA as associate professor of home management, Dr. Mize would continue to support this philosophy through her research in housing and household equipment and her innovative teaching style. She served on the faculty at the College of Home Economics for 22 years, serving as department head of the Housing and Home Management Department from 1959 to 1974. She also served as a project director for studies of housing with the Southern Regional Housing Project from 1954 to 1974, and was a frequent contributor to bulletins from the Georgia Agricultural Experiment Station. Mize served as the editor of several comprehensive historical works, including *The History of Home*

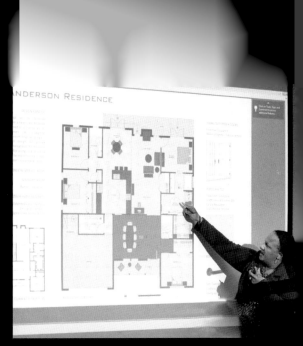

Economics at the University of Georgia, published in 1983. She was inducted into the FACS Honor Hall of Recognition in 2004.

Dr. Mize's mother, Leila Richie Mize, a pioneer extension leader and one of the first four district home demonstration agents named in Georgia, was inducted into the FACS Honor Hall of Recognition in 1981.

Today, students in the Textiles, Merchandising and Interiors Department who are

pursuing a major in furnishings and interiors focus on the interior design of residential environments, such as single- and multi-family housing, assisted living facilities, and hospitality, with an emphasis on kitchen and bath design to meet the changing needs of a diverse population. The program also provides a strong background in textile end-use and performance, and is accredited by the National Kitchen and Bath Association (NKBA).

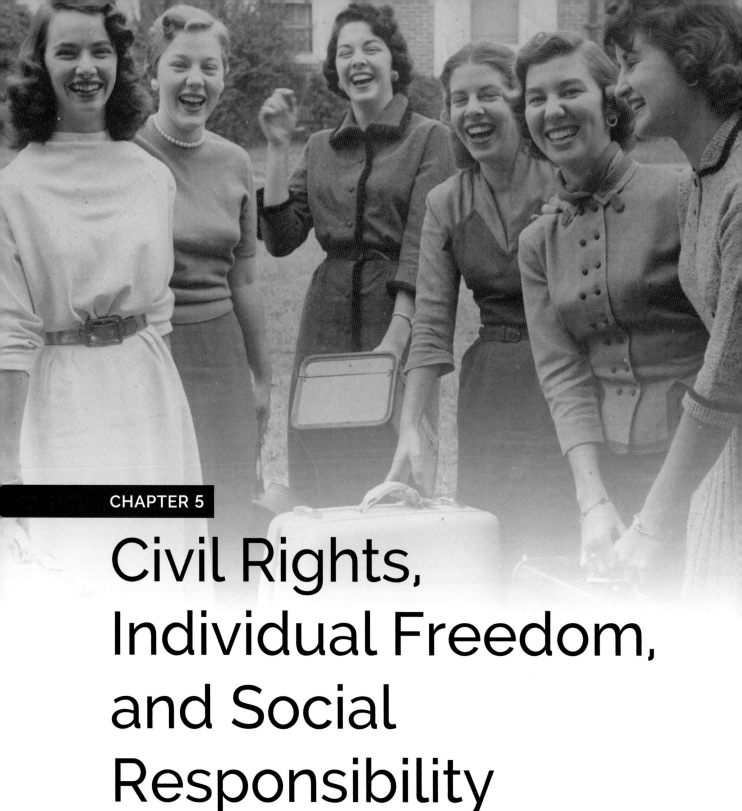

CHAPTER 5

Civil Rights, Individual Freedom, and Social Responsibility

1955–1969

With the landmark Supreme Court decision in 1954 outlawing all "separate, but equal" state laws, the civil rights movement gained momentum in the late 1950s and throughout the 1960s. Protests, marches, and demonstrations—peaceful and otherwise—are well documented throughout this period.

The role of women was also changing. Though many contributing factors can be sited, the growing array of modern conveniences gave women more time to pursue personal interests, including higher education and employment outside the home. Betty Friedan's *The Feminine Mystique* (1963) and other books helped bring this social transition into public view.

In the book *Remaking Home Economics* (2015), editor Sharon Y. Nickols and contributor Billie Collier report on the changing roles of women in society. "Women's roles in society continued to change over the next decades as increasing numbers of women, especially married women and mothers, entered the paid work force." Consequently, "in a little more than a generation (approximately 1945–1975), the size of the US employed female labor force more than doubled."

By the mid-1950s, interest in the study of traditional home economics subjects began to decline as women moved away from traditional homemaker roles. This trend would continue well into the 1960s. Schools of home economics, including UGA, were challenged to adapt their course work to meet the changing needs of current students, while appealing to new students in search of career opportunities.

TIMELINE

1955 – The Rock Eagle 4-H Center opens in Eatonton, Georgia. The center is funded in part by private funds, through the Georgia 4-H Foundation chartered in 1948, and with matching state funds pledged by Governor Herman Talmadge. The governor also volunteers skilled prison labor to construct the facility.

1956 – The tea room lab, opened in 1954 as a teaching center, is closed. Today, the space, Room 104, serves as a textiles research lab.

1956 – The Georgia Center for Continuing Education is completed thanks in part to a Kellogg Foundation grant. The center serves as a partner in the development and delivery of a variety of programs. Today it is one of eight units within the university's Office of Public Service and Outreach focused on serving Georgia and addressing vital issues important to the state and its citizens.

1957 – A Home Economics Day is held on January 31 with over 650 visitors, including high school and college students, teachers, and extension agents from across Georgia. Home Economics Days are designed to familiarize high school and junior college students with the School of Home Economics at UGA. The day includes tours of Dawson Hall, the nursery school, home management houses, and the freshmen women's dorm.

1959 – Pakistani graduate students Razia Khatoon, Jahan Khattak, and Mokhlese Mugharbel are enrolled in the foods and nutrition program. The students are supported by the Ford Foundation as part of the project to bring home economics to Pakistan. The project was managed by Dr. Maude Pye Hood from 1954 to 1957. The students graduate in 1962. Korean student Chung-Soon, recipient of a Georgia Rotary scholarship, majors in family development.

1959 – "Rocket to the Stars with Home Economics" is the theme of this year's Home Economics Day, held on January 30. The event draws more than a thousand students from across the state.

1960 – A textiles research lab is established in the physics building.

> **FACS FAST FACT**
>
> Research projects in 1960 emphasized:
> - Clothing and Textiles
> - Child Development
> - Family Economics
> - Family Relations
> - Nutrition
> - Housing and Management

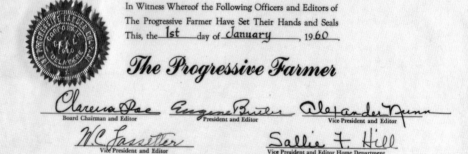

For Outstandingly Useful Services

Rendered to Her State and Especially to Its Rural People and Their Welfare and Progress

Dr. Mary Speirs

is Hereby Recognized as

WOMAN OF THE YEAR

In Service to Georgia Agriculture
for the year 1959

In Witness Whereof the Following Officers and Editors of
The Progressive Farmer Have Set Their Hands and Seals
This, the 1st day of January, 1960

The Progressive Farmer

Board Chairman and Editor   President and Editor   Vice President and Editor

Vice President and Editor   Vice President and Editor Home Department

1960 – *The Progressive Farmer* names Dean Mary Speirs "Woman of the Year" in recognition of her "outstanding useful services rendered to her state and especially to the rural people and their welfare and progress."

1961 – The University of Georgia admits its first African American students. Charlayne Hunter, the first female African American student, lives in Myers Hall. Among the first African Americans to graduate from the School of Home Economics were Cathy Dunaway (child development/mental retardation), Marian Turnipseed (clothing and textiles), and Bridget Weaver (dietetics) in 1976.

1961 – The Panel on Mental Retardation is established by President John F. Kennedy to evaluate the needs of individuals with developmental disabilities, and to develop strategies for public policy reform. A report by the panel, presented in 1963, laid the foundation for legislation to fund research, university-based diagnostic treatment clinics, and community centers for the care of people with developmental disabilities.

Legislation passed that year also provides funding for the training of special education teachers. In 1968, Eunice Kennedy Shriver, the president's sister, founded the Special Olympics to celebrate the achievements of athletes with disabilities. Today, more than 2.5 million children and adults, from 180 countries, participate in the event.

1962 – The biennial meeting of Phi Upsilon Omicron is held in Athens. Dean Maude Pye Hood is the national president.

1962 – A grant of more than $35,000 from the National Institute of Mental Health funds a program for the training of preschool center personnel for two more years. The nine-month training course, developed by the School of Home Economics, is offered through the Georgia Center for Continuing Education. Three hundred educators are enrolled in the course.

PHI UPSILON OMICRON

Phi Upsilon Omicron is open to membership to women in the Home Economics School who have maintained an 85 average or above and have shown leadership in campus activities and professional promise in the field of home economics. Officers are: Jolyn Chastain, Pres.; Sara Roberson, V.P.; Margie McIntyre, Sec.; Ann Willett, Treas.

First row: Jolyn Chastain, Glenda Kight, Carolyn Cadle, Barbara Lewis. *Second row:* Nancy Williams, Sheryl Allison, Ann Williams, Jenny Thrash, Margie McIntyre. *Third row:* Hilda Terry, Lynette Garrett, DiAnn Patillo, Sharon Hamner, Rite Watersm, Mary Stone, Ann Willett.

388

1964 – With the signing of the Civil Rights Act by President Lyndon Johnson, Georgia Cooperative Extension offices across the state become integrated. Early extension office maps depict both "white" and "negro" locations within four districts: Augusta, Savannah, Macon, and Atlanta.

1965 – A grant proposal for the construction of the Athens branch of the Georgia Retardation Center is approved. Intellectual disabilities becomes an area of study within the School of Home Economics. The Athens branch opens in 1969.

Home Demonstration Work

The aim of the home demonstration program is to stimulate the development of attractive, efficient, prosperous, satisfying farm homes in Georgia and to assist in solving the problems of rural life confronting the women and girls of the state. It is concerned with the economic and educational problems as well as the social and spiritual values of the home.

The projects of work undertaken were determined by the Director of Home Economics in conference with other state and district workers. The district agent guides the county agent in working out the program for an individual county. The county officials

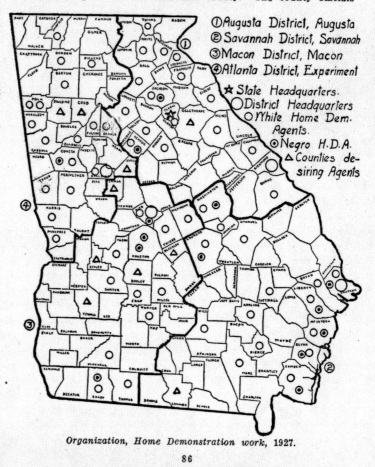

① Augusta District, Augusta
② Savannah District, Savannah
③ Macon District, Macon
④ Atlanta District, Experiment

★ State Headquarters.
◯ District Headquarters
◯ White Home Dem. Agents.
◉ Negro H.D.A.
△ Counties desiring Agents

Organization, Home Demonstration work, 1927.

86

1965 – Dr. William Caster, professor of food and nutrition, helps pioneer the discovery of the relationship between fatty acids and heart disease. Research indicates that a deficiency in essential fatty acids in a person's diet can be as detrimental to heart function as too much saturated fat. Dr. Caster also helped create a joint PhD program in nutrition with the Department of Animal Science.

1965 – UGA faculty members Dr. Elizabeth Sheerer and Margaret McPhaul serve as consultants to the US Office of Education for the development of "Child Centers," which soon after become the national Head Start program. According to the Georgia Head Start Association (GHSA), the program "was designed to help break the cycle of poverty by providing preschool children of low-income families with a comprehensive program to meet their emotional, social, health, nutritional, and psychological needs." Supervised by the US Office of Economic Opportunity, training courses are held on campus to prepare teachers for participation in the program. Head Start continues to serve low-income preschool children and families today.

1965 – In response to the growing number of older people and their diverse needs, the Older Americans Act (OAA) is passed. The UGA Institute on Gerontology is established the same year to focus on improving the health and quality of life of older adults in communities across Georgia.

1967 – The Institute on Human Development and Disability (IHDD) opens to create opportunities for people with disabilities. The institute, which works with individuals with disabilities, their family members, federal and state agencies, and service providers, is a member of the Association of University Centers on Disabilities. IHDD works with 67 universities and teaching hospitals across the country.

1966 – The State Training Office for Child Development is established to provide and coordinate training and assistance for Head Start programs located in 143 centers throughout Georgia. The office is focused on education, social services, parent involvement, nutrition, medical, dental health, mental health, career development, community involvement, volunteer and administration training, and technical assistance.

1967 – James W. Andrews, Jr., from Robinson, Georgia, becomes the first UGA graduate to receive a doctor of philosophy degree in human nutrition, the joint degree program established in 1965 by Dr. William Caster.

1968 – Peter Stegmayer is one of the first male graduates of the School of Home Economics with a major in diet and institution management. Jerry Joe Bigner of St. Simons, Georgia, earns a master of science degree in child development that year.

"Ever since I can remember I've been interested in foods, restaurants and the like. Some of the guys rib me about it but it doesn't bother me."

—Peter Stegmayer
Speaking to the Associated Press in February 1968

1969 – The Mental Retardation Center begins operations for 40 trainable and 40 educable mentally handicapped people to age 21.

1969 – The graduate degree of specialist in education is added.

1969 – Dr. Mary Speirs testifies before a Georgia House of Representatives committee studying hunger and malnutrition. She shares research that indicates eating too much of the wrong food is as harmful as eating too little. "Since the 1940s, the average American has become worse in his eating habits," Speirs told the committee. She went on to explain how research has demonstrated that the human body needs food from four basic groups every day: meats, vegetables and fruits, breads and cereals, and milk products.

Personal Journey – Maude Pye Hood

Beginning in 1951, the Ford Foundation provided grants to aid Pakistan in the development of key educational institutions and core competencies. Partnering with various universities, the foundation provided funds for foreign advisors, training of Pakistani institutional staff in the United States, and the purchase of equipment and materials. Among the pioneers was UGA School of Home Economics dean Maude Pye Hood, who spent three years in Pakistan working to establish a college of home economics.

A native of Talbot County in west central Georgia, Maude Pye Hood earned her bachelor's and master's degrees in home economics from the University of Georgia. She then earned her PhD from Iowa State University before joining the UGA faculty in 1937. Hood would spend 29 years with the School of Home Economics.

During her time overseas, from 1954 to 1957, Hood frequently corresponded with dear friends Mary and Edith Creswell. Her insightful observations, and humorous anecdotes, clearly demonstrate her sense of adventure and a commitment to the mission, all the while tempered by a heavy heart missing family, friends, and colleagues back home.

In one of her first letters home, Hood writes: "The first month has been an unusually busy one as there were pressing matters that had accumulated in the four months when there was no home economist here. Perhaps the biggest factor in all this is the Begum Liaquat Ali Khan leaves for the Netherlands in a few weeks. A Begum is a madam of distinction. Begum Liaquat is the President of the All-Pakistan-Woman's

Association, the organization that holds the Ford Foundation grant under which we are working and the college is being established. She has now been appointed the ambassador to the Netherlands. She has been the whole show in APWA, so if we want things to move we've got to get them moving before she takes leave."

Later, she writes: "Transportation. It's worth a trip over here to have Hussain, our driver, drive you from the airport. My hair is still standing on end. It literally is, whatever the cause may be! There are motor bikes, cycle rickshaws, horse drawn victorias, donkey carts, camel carts, jeeps, cars, trucks, and pedestrians all moving in many directions over the one narrow street. The camels delight me. They wear straps with the nicest-toned bells around their knees. As they trot rhythmically down the road with heads held high and a Mona Lisa smile, they amuse me to no end."

Hood continues this letter with: "This is Karachi's most delightful season, but I have really felt sorry for you people sweltering in the heat of Georgia while I enjoyed a wonderful sea breeze. Our office is air conditioned but AB (Alma Beth Clark) and I prefer to cut the air conditioning off, open the window and get the nice cool breeze. Even my ankles, knees (un-stockinged for economy) get cold. October, they say, will not be as cool because there's less breeze and April, May and June are the really hot months."

In a letter from October 1954, Hood writes: "I miss my friends and my family very much but I am having such an enjoyable and enriching experience I can't help being real happy to be here. I want you to know that I think of you and Miss E. often, very, very often, and I wish the best for each of you. Much love, Maude Pye."

In a letter dated December 1954, Hood describes how she is adapting to the local culture. "I'm so adjusted to Pakistan and its ways that I can sit on the floor and sop up curry with a chapati without having tears run down my cheeks," Hood wrote. "I've been to (three) Muslim weddings lately. The wedding ceremony is customarily followed by a dinner. The food was so rich with ghee and hot with curry & chill. I felt like a blow torch in an oil well when I finished eating."

In December 1956, as the journey home approaches, Hood puts the past year in perspective. "You have shared so many experiences with me here (in my mind) that I wish you could see the school and student body. The students remind me a lot of teenagers in my day – not nearly as sophisticated and self-sufficient as those of today. All in all it has been

a good year and I'm looking forward now to seeing the USA in June. Love, Pye."

Following her retirement in 1966, Maude Pye Hood returned to Pakistan for three additional years to serve as chief advisor to the program. A Pakistani burqa, donated by Hood, is part of the Historic Costume Collection. She was inducted into the FACS Honor Hall of Recognition in 1993.

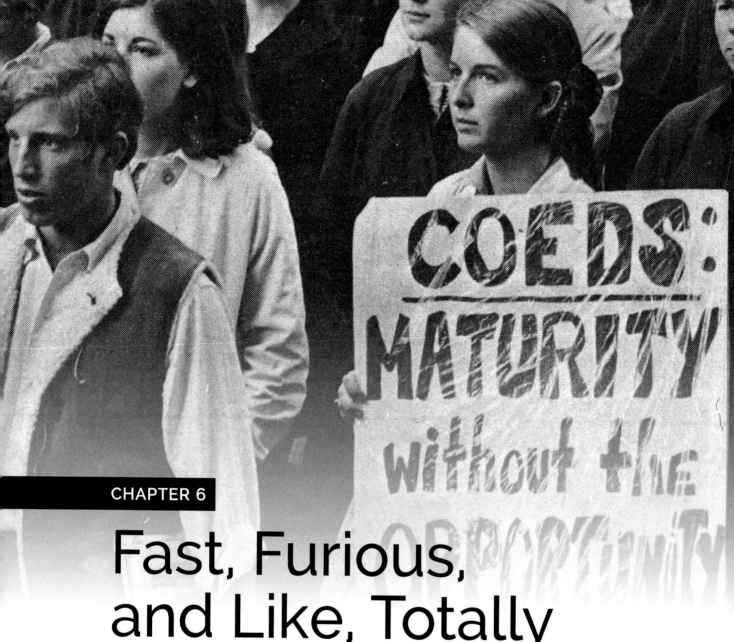

CHAPTER 6

Fast, Furious, and Like, Totally Awesome

1970–1989

Historical accounts of the 1970s and 1980s reveal a period of extraordinary growth driven by complex social and economic factors, polarizing political events, and the rapid development of technology. Both the Civil Rights and feminist movements of the 1960s continued to gain momentum, as did another generational revolt against everything "establishment." The mantra of the hippie movement, "Make love, not war," prompted, among other things, an increase in premarital sex and drug use. Other events of the era making headlines included the Vietnam War, Watergate, the 1973 Arab oil embargo, the Cold War, Reaganomics, Apple computers, the space race, the Tehran hostage crisis, and the Camp David

Accords. Richard Nixon, Gerald Ford, Jimmy Carter, Ronald Reagan, and George H. W. Bush all occupied the White House between 1970 and 1989.

College campuses across the country were frequently the scenes of marches, sit-ins, and other forms of protest. Students rallied together to make their voices heard on a number of fronts, including diversity, inclusion, government policy, and spending. University enrollment skyrocketed, nearly tripling from 1960 to 1970 at UGA. Students, especially women, were now focused on developing solid career paths and maximizing their employability. University curriculums needed to be updated and expanded, and faculty and administrators needed to be innovative and responsive to meet the ever-changing demands of the growing student population. These challenges were never more evident than within the UGA School of Home Economics. It is during these two decades that significant growth and change would occur.

On the occasion of her retirement as dean in 1991, Dr. Emily Quinn Pou summed up the achievements of this dynamic era. She wrote, "As faculty, we have made it possible for students to attain greater levels of specialization and to receive the preparation required for success in a variety of new fields, reflecting the mission of our profession to improve the quality of life. In doing so, however, we have moved our focus from individual and family living in the home to success in a variety of new arenas. We have provided our students with the skills necessary to be successful in the vastly more complex world that we face today."

TIMELINE

1970 – The Georgia Council on Developmental Disabilities (DD Council), which reports to the US Department of Health and Human Services' Administration on Intellectual and Developmental Disabilities, is created. Its mission is to "promote public policy that creates an integrated community life for persons with developmental disabilities."

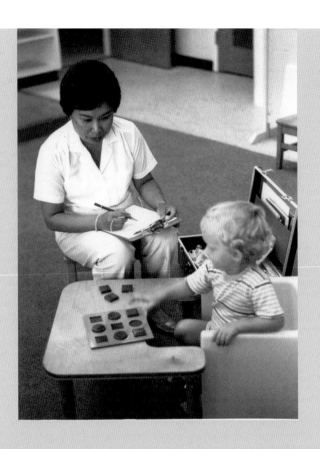

1970 – The new Child and Family Development Center is completed. The facility, built with funds from the US Office of Education and the Georgia Education Authority, includes laboratories for the study of infants, toddlers, preschool children, and kindergarteners.

1971 – Dr. Mary Speirs retires as dean on June 30. Dr. Elizabeth Sheerer serves as acting dean until August 15, when Dr. Emily Quinn (later Pou) is named dean of the School of Home Economics. Quinn comes to the school from North Carolina State University, where she is a professor of education and state leader of extension training.

1971 – The new Dawson Hall Annex is occupied. The 26,228-square-foot, fully air-conditioned addition provides classrooms, laboratories, and offices for the Departments of Clothing and Textiles, Foods and Nutrition, and Housing and Home Management.

1972 – Four new introductory courses are offered, one each from the Departments of Child and Family Development, Clothing and Textiles, Foods and Nutrition, and Housing and Home Management. The four courses, totaling 20 credit hours, replace the 51 hours of core credits previously required of all home economics students. This significant change allows students to spend more time focused on their individual areas of specialization.

1973 – The Child and Family Development Center is renamed the Margaret E. McPhaul Child and Family Development Center. The facility, together with the Dawson Hall Annex, is dedicated in May.

Each of these new structures provides the laboratories in which new knowledge may be generated and the application of that knowledge tested in fostering the development of individuals and professionals whose dedication will be the enhancement of the quality of living for the citizenry of Georgia.

—Dean Emily Quinn, *Athens Banner-Herald*, April 23, 1973

1973 – The Public Service Unit is established through a joint effort among the School of Home Economics, the Georgia Center for Continuing Education, and the Cooperative Extension Service. The unit provides continuing educational programs for professionals and paraprofessionals in home economics and related fields. The unit grows from one program specialist in 1973 to nine in 1990.

1974 – Drs. Sharon Price and Elizabeth Sheerer of the Department of Child and Family Development are awarded the first Outstanding Teacher of the Year Awards.

1974 – Myers Hall, named for UGA home economics graduate and Soule Hall housemother Jennie Belle Myers, is the site of the nation's largest streaking event. Approximately a thousand naked students were led by a Lady Godiva-inspired woman riding on a white horse.

BRUCE
PUBLIC SCHOOL
1973-74
ROOM 8

1974 – Georgia begins funding of public kindergarten programs. The School of Home Economics and the College of Education team up to help meet the demand for certified kindergarten teachers.

1974 – Dr. Jessie J. Mize retires as head of the Department of Housing, Home Management and Furnishings, a position she held for 15 years.

FACS FAST FACT

Majors in the School of Home Economics in 1975:
    Department of Child & Family Development
- Child Development
- Child Development – Mental Retardation
- Child Development – Early Childhood Education
- Family Development
- Child & Family Development

Department of Clothing & Textiles
- Clothing and Textiles
- Fashion Merchandising

Department of Housing, Home Management & Furnishings
- Consumer Economics and Family
- Management
- Housing
- Home Economics and Art
- Home Economics and Interior Design
- Furnishings and Interiors

Department of Foods & Nutrition
- Experimental Foods
- Nutrition Science
- Dietetics and Institutional Management
- Community Nutrition

Home Economics Education

Home Economics and Journalism

1976 – The first PhD program in the School of Home Economics, in child and family development, is approved by the board of regents. Five students enter the program in September. Nine additional students are admitted the following year. Lynda Henley Walters receives the first doctorate awarded through the college in 1978.

"From its inception, it has been the philosophy of the faculty that the PhD should develop leaders for the future. It does so by providing outstanding education, supporting the strengths of students, and developing collegial relationships that prepare students for professional roles."

—Dr. Lynda Walters

Dr. Walters served as associate dean from 1982 to 1991.

1976 – A new major within the Department of Foods and Nutrition, food service management, is added. The program places emphasis on the managerial aspects of food service. Graduates are prepared for employment in restaurants, school food service, and industrial food service positions.

1977 – The Hazel and Gene Franklin Scholarship Fund is established. The fund provides an annual grant of $250 to one home economics graduate student and one home economics undergraduate student based on academic achievement, leadership qualities, and related activities.

"Alumni are particularly important to our school's development," Dean Pou told the *Athens Banner-Herald*. "The interest and support of alumni such as Mr. and Mrs. Franklin do much to strengthen and upgrade the educational opportunities our school can offer."

1977 – The Housing, Home Management and Furnishings Department becomes Housing, Home Management and Consumer Economics Department. According to Dr. Anne Sweaney, the name was recommended by the American Home Economics Association Accreditation team. The department head at the time, Dr. James Montgomery, proposed Housing, Family Management and Consumer Economics.

1977 – The Home Economics Alumni Association is formed. The first annual meeting is held in October of the following year.

. . . .

1978 – An anonymous gift of $50,000 to the School of Home Economics is made; $40,000 is designated for the purchase of research and instructional equipment with the remainder set aside for seminars to benefit both faculty and students.

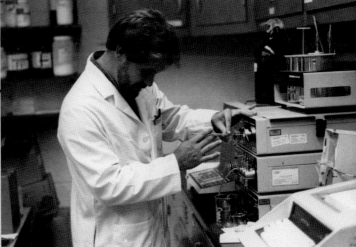

1978 – The School of Home Economics becomes the College of Home Economics.

1978 – The Gerontology Center is established to coordinate and expand the university's programs on aging.

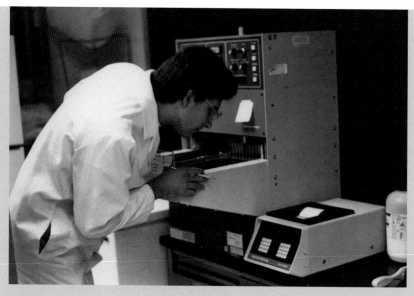

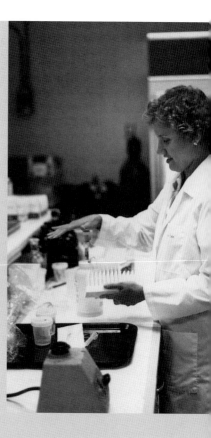

1979 – Numerous research grants and contracts are awarded to the college from the National Institutes of Health, the National Meat Board, the Minnesota Beef Council, the American Diabetes Association, Weight Watchers, USDA-SEA, the Appalachian Regional Commission, and the Georgia Department of Offender Rehabilitation. The total is more than $1.1 million.

1979 – The UGA Student Home Economics Association (UGA/SHEA) hosts an orientation session for new students to familiarize them with the various degrees, careers, and clubs within the College of Home Economics.

FACS FAST FACT
Starting Salaries for Home Economics Graduates in 1980:
- $10,500 for a Bachelor of Science
- $12,000 for a Master of Science
- $15,000 for a PhD

1979 – The Dean's Aide program is initiated. Six students are selected to assist the Office of the Dean in recruitment and public relations activities. Today, FACS Ambassadors continue this important work.

• •

1980 – The UGA College of Home Economics Alumni Association establishes the first awards program. Five awards are given: Appreciation of Home Economics, The Creswell Award, Distinguished Alumni Award, Pacesetter Award, and Honor Hall of Recognition. Since its creation, 28 distinguished individuals have been inducted into the Honor Hall of Recognition.

FACS FAST FACT

Honor Hall of Recognition Recipients, 1980–1989:
- Mary Creswell
- Leila Richie Mize
- Asia Elizabeth Todd
- Margaret McPhaul
- Dr. Mary Speirs
- Janette McGarity Barber
- Eleanor Pryor
- Leolene Chapman Montgomery
- Leonora Anderson
- Francis Chapman

1980 – A PhD program in foods and nutrition is added. Six students are enrolled in the program. John McNamara receives the first doctoral degree in March 1982. His foods and nutrition hood still hangs in his office.

"My major professor, Roy Martin, had just moved there, and we were temporarily in Animal Sciences while the new PhD program was under review. Moving from a very large established program (at Penn State) to a brand new one, at a university that, at that time, had a smaller presence in nutrition, animal sciences and related fields, it was a challenge to be unsure exactly which "way to jump"; stay in Animal Sciences (at PSU) or move to a new program. BUT, having a say in the structure of the new program and working with dedicated other students was very rewarding."

—Dr. John P. McNamara
Emeritus Professor of Animal Sciences, Washington State University

1980 – Dr. Roy Martin, professor of foods and nutrition, receives a $36,000, five-year grant to continue his search for ways to control obesity and diabetes. "The number of problems that can stem from obesity is shocking," Martin told the Athens Banner-Herald in February 1980. "Among them are diabetes, heart attacks, gall bladder problems, kidney stones, gout, and some types of cancer."

1980 – Dr. Martin was inducted into the Honor Hall of Recognition in 2016. He currently serves as an adjunct professor at the University of California-Davis and as a visiting professor at Western Human Nutrition Research Center, an Agricultural Resource Service of the USDA.

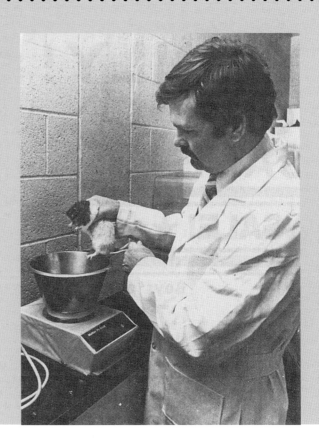

1981 – Dr. Anne Sweaney accepts a part-time position with the Southern Regional Housing Research Project sponsored by the Agricultural Experiment Station. The following year, she earns a tenure-track assistant professor of housing position. Widely known and published in the field of housing, her research interests include the effect of public policy on housing for families and consumers, housing needs of older adults, and the role of technology in adapting housing for the life span.

One day I got a call from Dean Emily Pou. She said, 'Would you come over and help Dr. (James) Montgomery with this housing research project?' The first position was a part-time temporary assistant professor. That's where it all started. I came for a day and stayed for a fabulous career.

—Dr. Anne Sweaney,
Josiah Meigs Distinguished Teaching Professor and
Professor Emerita

1982 – The first computer lab is established for use by students and faculty in the College of Home Economics.

1983 – Children with developmental delays are mainstreamed into the regular children's laboratory programs at the McPhaul Child and Family Development Center. Positive outcomes include increasing student understanding of these children while providing a way for the children to learn social skills and acceptance.

1983 –The Legislative Aide program, supported by private donors, is established. Spearheaded by Dean Emily Pou, Dr. Anne Sweaney, and Dr. Jessie Mize, the program provides a stipend to students assigned to a Georgia senator or representative during the legislative session. A Congressional Aide program in Washington, DC, is added in 1985. Dr. Mize is among the first contributors.

"These are home economics majors finding out firsthand what was happening at the (state) capitol, and helping with those issues," Dr. Sweaney said. "They had a different view of what family (and) consumer sciences could contribute to the issues there."

I actually got to see up close and personal the decisions that policy makers have to make and more importantly I got to see the impact of research and service through the Cooperative Extension Service. And what a difference that organization makes in 159 counties in Georgia. So during those three months of the Georgia General Assembly, I had the opportunity to help Representative (Hugh) Logan collect information, develop policy briefs and work with his constituents, certainly from Athens Clarke County but all across the state of Georgia.

—Dr. Debbie Redeker Phillips, 1985–1986 Legislative Aide,
President, The Quadrillion, Stockbridge, Georgia

1983 – The first male students take up residence in a home management house as part of their course work in home management and consumer economics. Josh Borden is the first male student to earn a degree in housing. Darrell Jackson and Michael Girardeau are the first men to earn degrees in consumer economics.

1984 – Dawson Hall and Speirs Hall, formally known as the Dawson Hall Annex, are dedicated during the spring Home Economics Alumni weekend. Among the additions to Dawson Hall is an impressive entrance with three-story columns and a balcony. The columns are affectionately known as "Pou's Pillars."

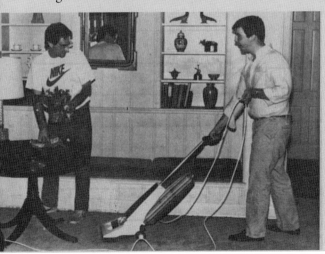

The History of HOME ECONOMICS at the University of Georgia

1985 – *The History of Home Economics at the University of Georgia*, edited by Dr. Jessie J. Mize, is published. The book chronicles the teaching, research, and public service of home economics at UGA from 1911 to 1981.

1985 – A survey is conducted of the faculty to determine the continued appropriateness of the name, "Home Economics." When asked, "Shall we engage in consideration of a name change for the College of Home Economics?" . . . more than 80 percent said yes.

1985 – Georgia legislators, in both the state senate and house of representatives, adopt resolutions honoring the outstanding leadership of Dean Emily Quinn Pou. Among her many contributions were the installation of a computer lab within the college, the establishment of student scholarships, the attracting of nationally recognized faculty, and the development of the innovative Legislative Aide and Congressional Aide programs.

1985 – A law passed in July requiring the licensure of marriage and family therapists prompts creation of the marriage and family therapy post graduate program. The following year, the PhD program is accredited by the American Association for Marriage and Family Therapy.

FACS FAST FACT

Over $1 million in grants and awards is received in 1986. Contributing organizations include:
- Research Triangle
- Eli Lilly
- Genentech, Inc.
- National Kidney Foundation
- Governor's Office of Energy Resources
- US Department of Health and Human Services
- National Institute of Mental Health
- National Science Foundation
- United States Army
- Army Research Institute
- United States Navy
- Kellogg Foundation

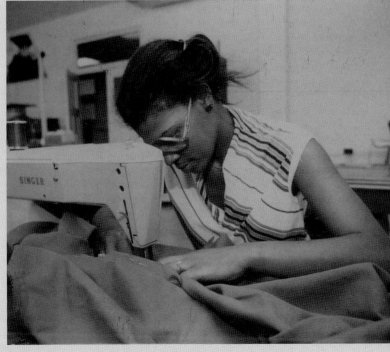

1985 – The Department of Clothing and Textiles becomes the Department of Textiles, Merchandising and Interiors.

1986 – The home management residence requirement for students in the Department of Housing and Consumer Economics is discontinued. The houses are converted into much-needed office space for the college.

"The increasing diversity of the student population played a role in discontinuing the 'live-in' aspect of the course, as did the difficulties of adapting the experience to the realities of today's families. Today, far greater emphasis is placed on management research and far less emphasis is placed on a hands-on, laboratory approach."

—Dr. James Walters, Professor Emeritus and Editor, *Decades of Progress: 1971–1991*

1986 – The USDA Fellowship Program for PhD students provides funding for research in obesity, diabetes, trace minerals, heart disease, hypertension, food product development, and the regulation of food intake.

1987 – A request to the board of regents to change the name of the College of Home Economics is returned to University president Charles K. Knapp for further study. The proposed new name, College of Human Ecology (used by similar institutions including Cornell University, Michigan State University, Kansas State University, University of Maryland, and the University of Tennessee), is denied.

1988 – A dietary managers program is developed and approved by the Dietary Managers Association.

1988 – Textiles, merchandising and interiors (TMI) students participate in the UGA Studies Abroad program in Cortona, Italy. Established in 1968 by the UGA Art Department, TMI students attend classes and tour both textile manufacturing facilities and an annual trade show of furniture and accessories from worldwide manufacturers. Fashion merchandising and interiors majors participate in the program in 1989.

1988 – UGA is designated a Regional Research Center by the National Association of Home Builders/National Research Center. The center will focus on consumers of housing and the policies that affect them rather than the engineering aspects being studied at 16 other research centers across the country.

1988 – Significant research into the physical chemistry of indigo dyeing is begun by Dr. J. Nolan Etters with the Department of Textiles, Merchandising and Interiors. Results would illustrate how variations in the dyeing process of denim jean fabric make blue jeans so comfortable and actually improve with age. At the time, no other American university was pursuing such research.

1989 – The UGA Program for Persons with Developmental Disabilities is moved from the College of Education to the College of Home Economics. Dr. Zolinda Stoneman, professor of child and family development, is named director.

1989 – Video teleconferencing is used by the Public Service Section of the College of Home Economics to facilitate meetings with the Georgia Cooperative Extension Service, the Dairy and Food Nutrition Council, and the State Department of Education. Topics include "Teenage Sexuality," "Nutrition and Aging," and "Eating for the Health of It."

1989 – Despite rigorous objections from some alumni, the faculty of the College of Home Economics recommends that the name of the college be changed to Family and Consumer Sciences. A survey of student preferences supports this recommendation. More than 71 percent of those responding said changing the name of the college would increase the value of their degrees. Kathy Palmer, a 1976 home economics graduate and at the time a Swainsboro attorney, leads the opposition. "Does 'family and consumer sciences' portray a different image than 'home economics'?" Palmer is quoted in an article published by the *Atlanta Journal* and the *Atlanta Constitution* in November 1989. "With no consistency on a national basis, we've not helped change or update the image, just confuse it."

FACS FAST FACT
Enrollment:
   1970 – 530 Students
   1976 – 781 Students
   1981 – 789 Students
   1988 – 846 Students

Personal Journey – Eleanor Pryor

ederal legislation authored by Senator Richard B. Russell of Georgia in 1946 provided permanent status and funding for the National School Lunch Program. The legislation reads in part, "It is hereby declared to be the policy of Congress, as a measure of national security, to safeguard the health and well-being of the Nation's children and to encourage the domestic consumption of nutritious agricultural commodities and other food, by assisting the States, through grants-in-aid and other means, in providing an adequate supply of food and other facilities for the establishment, maintenance, operation and expansion of nonprofit school lunch programs."

Considered one of the early champions of the program in Georgia was 1933 UGA home economics graduate Eleanor Pryor. Following a brief turn teaching in rural schools, Pryor joined the Georgia Department of Education as assistant state supervisor of the National School Lunch Program. In 1946, she was named state supervisor of the $30 million program, a position she would hold until her death in 1961 at the age of 49.

Pryor was first nominated for the College of Home Economics Honor Hall of Recognition in 1984. At the time, Josephine Martin, director of the Local Systems Support Division, Georgia Department of Education, wrote of Pryor: "She led in the improvement of lunchroom kitchens and equipment as new schools were built all over the state. She worked with state, regional and national organizations to secure nutritious school lunches and improved the standard of sanitation and food quality. With her low voice, encouragement, leadership qualities and bright eyes, she contributed to millions of healthier school children in Georgia and across the nation." Pryor would be inducted into the Honor Hall of Recognition in 1986.

According to those who knew her, she possessed four of the basic characteristics of a leader: commitment, competence, concern, and character.

During the recognition presentation, Martin said: "She was committed to education and to nutrition. She believed the school lunch program would help safeguard the health and well-being of the nation's children. Miss Pryor never stopped being a teacher. Her educational philosophy and understanding of the teaching-learning process permeated her administration and management of the school lunch program. She had concern. She was concerned about the people with whom she worked. She inspired those of us who worked with her to do our best. Eleanor was the epitome of integrity. She was fair in all her dealings, and that was a tough role when dealing with nearly 200 school superintendents and more than 1,800 schools. She always followed through on her promises. You could count on Miss Pryor. She was a true leader."

In another tribute, Dr. Louise McBee, acting vice president for academic affairs, said: "Eleanor Pryor was allotted a relatively short lifespan, but in the course of 49 years, she burned an indelible imprint on countless lives as well as on the way in which the state of Georgia sought to provide resources for better lives among its citizens. We recall her today with admiration and affection, and we add her name to the Honor Hall of Recognition in deep appreciation for who she was and what she did."

According to USDA data for 2015, the latest year for which confirmed data are available, more than 100,000 schools and institutions are serving lunches to more than 30 million students each day. In Georgia, more than 1.1 million lunches are served daily by over 2,000 schools and institutions.

CHAPTER 7

Knowledge for Real Life

1990–2007

From the end of the Cold War and apartheid in South Africa to the creation of the European Union. From numerous battlegrounds abroad to the war on terrorism delivered to our doorstep on September 11, 2001. From dial-up internet service and chunky mobile phones to broadband, Blackberries, and iPhones. From AOL and Google to Facebook and YouTube. Without question, the social and economic landscape, both on a global and national level, was changing rapidly during the 1990s and early 2000s.

The Olympic Games came to Atlanta in 1996, catapulting the city, and the state of Georgia, onto the international stage. UGA would host a number of events, including volleyball, rhythmic gymnastics, and soccer. The US women's soccer team would win their first gold medal in Sanford Stadium on August 1.

On campus, baby boomers gave way to Generation X—students born between 1965 and 1984. Later, the first Generation Y, or Millennials, would begin to dot the landscape, bringing with them a distinctive set of behaviors and priorities. Advancements in technology would drive FACS course revisions, as the use of computers as integrated tools in the classroom approached 90 percent. Two periods of recession, in 1990 and 2001, would create economic challenges for the college.

Branding a new identity for the College of Family and Consumer Sciences took center stage early in the 1990s. A new name, a new look, and a new slogan—Knowledge for Real Life—would help chart the course for the future.

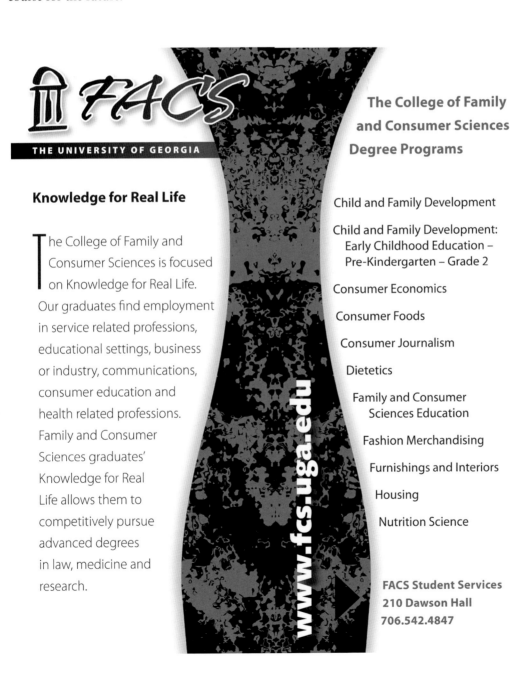

FACS

THE UNIVERSITY OF GEORGIA

Knowledge for Real Life

The College of Family and Consumer Sciences is focused on Knowledge for Real Life. Our graduates find employment in service related professions, educational settings, business or industry, communications, consumer education and health related professions. Family and Consumer Sciences graduates' Knowledge for Real Life allows them to competitively pursue advanced degrees in law, medicine and research.

The College of Family and Consumer Sciences Degree Programs

Child and Family Development

Child and Family Development: Early Childhood Education – Pre-Kindergarten – Grade 2

Consumer Economics

Consumer Foods

Consumer Journalism

Dietetics

Family and Consumer Sciences Education

Fashion Merchandising

Furnishings and Interiors

Housing

Nutrition Science

www.fcs.uga.edu

FACS Student Services
210 Dawson Hall
706.542.4847

TIMELINE

1990 – Emotions heat up once again on both sides of the college's name-change argument. The Coordinating Committee in Opposition to Name Change encourages College of Home Economics alumni to voice their opinions against the proposed name change to the board of regents and state senators and representatives. "The College of Home Economics has been able to modernize and improve its program of work through the modification and addition of majors within the degree structure. This committee feels that modifications at this level, not at the level of (the) name of the academic unit, can effectively facilitate the goals and objectives of the dean and faculty."

1990 – A written campaign in support of the name change is championed by Dr. Lynda Henley Walters, associate dean for research and instruction. In a letter to the board of regents, she writes, "Prospective employers, upon learning about the subject matter taught in home economics, have asked why we retain the name. They have said that they believe that the stereotype associated with home economics makes it difficult for students to obtain employment."

1990 – In a letter to UGA president Charles Knapp, dated June 13, 1990, Anne Flowers, vice chancellor for academic affairs, writes, "The Board of Regents, at its meeting June 13, 1990, approved your request to change the name of the College of Home Economics to College of Family and Consumer Sciences, effective July 1, 1990."

1990 – The PhD in textile sciences is approved. Miaolin Hou and Renita Jinkins are the first two students admitted to the program.

TO: Home Economics Graduate and Undergraduate Students

LET'S CONTROL OUR <u>OWN</u> FUTURE, NOT LET ALUMNI who graduated in the 60's and before!

We need a new name. Let's not allow the alumni to influence the nam change issue. We cannot allow ourselves to be STEREOTYPED AND OUTDATED, we must keep step with the changing world. The presen students need to take an active role in the name change process. We the ones who will be affected.

To find out how you can help, contact Markita Grant.

THIS IS A SERIOUS ISSUE and now is the TIME!

FACS FAST FACT
Honor Hall of Recognition Recipients, 1990–2007:
- Eddye B. Ross
- Montine Jackson
- Gwen Brooks O'Connell
- Dr. Maude Pye Hood
- Dr. Emily Quinn Pou
- Dr. Jessie Julia Mize
- Dr. James Walters
- Dr. Wanda Grogan

1991 – FACS Parents' Day is held in February. Parents and family of current students and prospective students spend the day touring campus facilities and learning more about the college.

1991 – Dean Emily Quinn Pou retires after serving the college for 20 years.

1991 – The UGA College of Agriculture (long a collaborative partner of the College of Family and Consumer Sciences as the face of the state's land-grant mission of teaching, research, and service through extension) becomes the College of Agricultural and Environmental Sciences (CAES). The name change reflects a growing emphasis on the environment and sustainability within the agricultural community.

1991 – UGA's Affiliated Program for Persons with Developmental Disabilities is administratively reorganized to function as a separate unit within the College of FACS. The program expands its contributions to the instructional, research, and service missions of the university through a 41 percent increase in external funding.

1991 – Sharon Y. Nickols is named dean of the college. During the 15 years she served as dean, degree programs were strengthened, study abroad programs were initiated, research productivity increased as new faculty joined the college, the Leadership FACS retreat was initiated, a position for development and external relations was created, and student enrollment increased dramatically.

It fulfilled every desire that I had here at the University of Georgia, to be in this environment, while the university was growing. Our students were vibrant, excited, had great career opportunities, the faculty was cohesive. I wanted to create an environment where we worked as a team, and I think we were successful with that.

—Dr. Sharon Y. Nickols, Dean and Professor Emerita
Oral History, August 2017, reflecting on her years as dean

1991 – All three floors of Dawson Hall are connected to the campus broadband for electronic communication. Access by all computer laboratories, faculty offices, and secretarial workstations is completed by spring 1992. Associate Deans Drs. Lynda Walters and Jan Hathcote coordinate implementation of these important initiatives.

1992 – The first student leadership development retreat, part of the Leadership FACS program, is held during the fall quarter. The retreat is designed to develop student leaders' ability to communicate effectively about the mission of the college, and to help build confidence and enthusiasm for the leadership paths they've chosen. The program celebrated 25 years in 2017.

1992 – The first College Convocation is held to recognize FACS graduates, faculty, and special guests. Graduates, family, and friends are invited to attend the ceremony. The College Convocation continues today as a cherished tradition.

1992 – The first group of students completes the London Study Abroad Program under the guidance of Dr. Anne Sweaney.

(We were) providing students with opportunities that they couldn't get just from the classroom, outside opportunities like the D.C. study tour, the London Program, the legislative aide program. These were home economics majors finding out firsthand what was happening. They had a different view of what family and consumer science could contribute.

—Dr. Anne Sweaney,
Josiah Meigs Distinguished Teaching Professor and
Professor Emerita
Oral History, August 2017

1992 – The Family Solutions Program, a collaborative effort between the Department of Child and Family Development and the Georgia Juvenile Court System, is founded to help youth and their families find solutions to help prevent repeat criminal offenses. Dr. William Quinn, associate professor and director of the marriage and family therapy program, is co-author of the initial intervention model. By 1998, the rate of re-offending behavior for youths in Athens-Clarke County who complete the program stood at 39 percent, compared with 61 percent for youths who do not complete the program.

1992 – The Undergraduate Studies Office becomes the Office of Student Services to more accurately reflect the scope of services provided to FACS students.

FACS FAST FACT
Innovative Courses Offered between 1990 and 2007:
- Management for Disadvantaged Families
- Selection, Use, and Care of Household Equipment
- Principles of Family Finance
- Family Demographics and Policy
- Advanced Housing Theories

1993 – The position of director of development is created.

"Serving as the FACS Director of Development was truly a career highlight for me. I came at a time when the Home Economics versus Family and Consumer Sciences name change was still very fresh. There was very little culture of philanthropy for the FACS alumni, yet we had big dreams that needed private funding. We recognized our characteristics and worked with them for the best outcome. I take pride in being a part of the 'early years' of development and helping to institutionalize the pride and importance of giving back to our alma mater."

—Katrina Bowers, BSHE '86 Consumer Economics, FACS Director of Development, 1996–2011

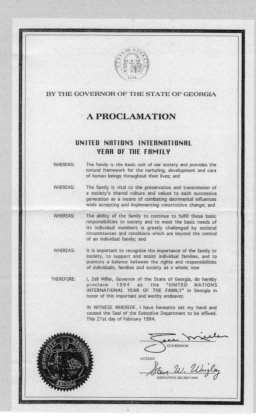

1994 – The United Nations declares 1994 the "International Year of the Family." FACS, together with its partners in the Georgia Coalition of Family and Consumer Sciences Professionals, worked with the Georgia General Assembly to develop and pass a resolution to designate the "International Year of the Family" in Georgia. Governor Zell Miller signed a proclamation which states in part, "It is important to recognize the importance of the family to society, to support and assist individual families, and to promote a balance between the rights and responsibilities of individuals, families and society as a whole."

1994 – In recognition of the "International Year of the Family," "Issues Facing Families" is among the programs led by the college held across the state. Dean Sharon Y. Nickols publishes the article "The Family: Smallest Democracy at the Heart of Society." In it, she writes, "The family—as an individual unit and as a social institution—is the state where tradition and modernity play a continuous tug of war. As family patterns transform, research will help governments and families respond and adjust more effectively to shifting political, economic and social forces."

1994 – The housing and consumer economics PhD program is approved. Six students enroll for the fall semester. By 2007, enrollment has increased to 10.

1994 – The American Home Economics Association (AHEA), founded in 1909, becomes the American Association of Family and Consumer Sciences (AAFCS). Today, the organization continues its commitment to "providing leadership and support to professionals whose work assists individuals, families, and communities in making informed decisions about their well-being, relationships, and resources to achieve optimal quality of life."

1994 – A new state initiative, the Consortium for Competitiveness for the Apparel, Carpet, and Textile Industry (CCACTI), provides a new source of support for research funding and graduate training in the FACS Textiles, Merchandising and Interiors Department.

1994 – Dr. William Flatt steps down as dean of the College of Agricultural and Environmental Sciences and joins the Department of Foods and Nutrition faculty of FACS. Since joining the college, Flatt has established three endowed scholarships, faculty awards, and two endowed professorships. He is a member of the prestigious "1785 Society," which recognizes cumulative gifts of $1 million or more. Today, Dr. Flatt continues to be an esteemed presence in Dawson Hall.

As an undergraduate, I received 12 scholarships that made it possible for me to go to college. That's one reason I feel fortunate to be able to "give back" to help other students achieve their goals to obtain a higher education.

—Dr. William Flatt

1995 – FACS launches its first web pages. The college is the third to establish a presence on the internet behind the University of Georgia website and the UGA Grady College of Journalism and Mass Communication.

" I had the first email in Dawson Hall. (People) thought I was crazy. I said, 'You just wait. Any minute now you are going to have your own address. You're going to have your own website.' The students remember this, the ones that I'm in touch with. They'll say, 'I remember when you came back from that conference and you said this World Wide Web is coming.'"

—Dr. Anne Sweaney
Josiah Meigs Distinguished Teaching Professor and Professor Emerita
Oral History, August 2017

1995 – The Statewide Independent Living Council of Georgia (SILC) is founded to promote equal participation of people with disabilities in their communities, and to increase the supports and services necessary for people with disabilities to find independent living opportunities.

1995 – The Glenn and Helen Burton "Feeding the Hungry Scholarship Fund" is endowed at $100,000. The fund supports one doctoral student in both FACS and CAES. The first scholarships are awarded in 1996. The field at UGA's Sanford Stadium, and putting greens across the south, are just some of the many beneficiaries of Dr. Burton's well-documented turf and forage hybrid development. Helen Burton, a dietetics graduate, directed the Meals on Wheels program in Tifton, Georgia.

1995 – A board of visitors is assembled to help advance the programs of the college. Composed of leaders in business and industry, state agency heads, practitioners, entrepreneurs, and private organization administrators, their mission is "to support and advance the College of Family and Consumer Sciences in its instructional research, and public service components to improve the human condition."

1996 – With the establishment of the college's web server, FACS receives permission from the Atlanta Committee for the Olympic Games to publish the Olympic volunteer newsletter, *Athens '96 Volunteer Voice.*

1997 – The UGA Office of International Education sponsors a new International Fellow Program. Dr. Patricia Hunt-Hurst is one of eight faculty members selected. Hunt-Hurst is a dress and fashion historian specializing in African American dress and textile history. Since 1996, she has been actively involved in study abroad programs in London and Ghana, offering unique educational experiences to students interested in adding a global perspective to their academic studies.

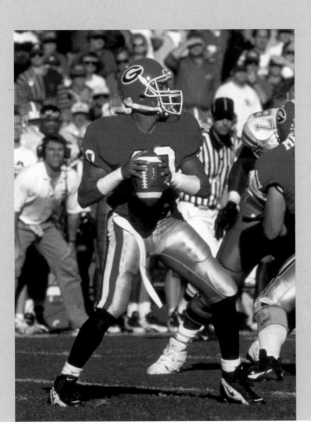

1998 – The University of Georgia completes the transition from a quarterly system to a semester system, allowing for core curriculum alignment among the 34 schools within the University System of Georgia. The semester system also helps ensure that students can graduate in four years. The FACS process for curriculum conversion has been a top priority for several years leading up to the conversion.

1998 – Hines Ward, Jr., a 1998 FACS graduate and Georgia Bulldogs wide receiver, is drafted by the Pittsburgh Steelers in the third round of the NFL draft. Ward would remain with the Steelers for 14 years until his retirement from professional football in 2012.

1998 – Computer-aided design (CAD) software is added to FACS computers for the teaching of furnishings and interiors students.

1998 – Emily Quinn Pou, former dean of the college, dies at the age of 69.

"Dean Pou made extraordinary contributions to her academic field and to the University of Georgia. The national stature of the College of Family and Consumer Sciences she led so well for 20 years is directly attributable to her vision and determination. The University will forever be grateful for her lifetime of devotion to its academic programs."

—Dr. Michael F. Adams
President, University of Georgia

1998 – An innovative program known as "Better Brains for Babies" is formed and led by FACS Extension faculty to share the latest research on early brain development. The objective is to "maximize Georgia's brain power." Fourteen public and private organizations from across the state, including FACS, contribute to the initial model.

1999 – The Nutrition Intervention Lab establishes Lovin' Spoonfuls/Cucharadas Amorosas, a video-based program to teach Latino mothers how to provide their children with more nutritious food. Peer educators, known and trusted within the Latino community, serve as course facilitators.

1999 – The Emily Quinn Pou Professional Achievement Award is established to recognize an alumnus who has attained substantial achievements and is in the midpoint of his/her career. Kathy Stephens Palmer, a 1976 family and development graduate, receives the inaugural award. Today, Palmer is the chief judge of the Middle Circuit of the 8th Superior Court District of Georgia. She was first elected in 2000.

2000 – Twenty-two housing and consumer economics students participate in the six-week study abroad program in London. Students participate in work experience and directed research courses. The program is coordinated through the American Institute for Foreign Study (AIFS) London and is open to all majors.

2001 – Dr. Jessie Julia Mize dies at the age of 90. In addition to her numerous academic achievements and contributions, Dr. Mize is also remembered as a dedicated financial supporter of the college. One area of special interest is the Legislative Aide program, founded in 1984. Her estate provides for an annual stipend in perpetuity. An additional endowment, in remembrance of Glenn Wilson "Jack" Ellard, clerk of the Georgia House of Representatives for 33 years, is received in 2005.

Edna Ellard, right, with Secretary of State Cathy Cox

2001 – The FACS Housing and Demographic Research Center conducts a comprehensive study of housing in the state of Georgia. The study is part of an effort by Lieutenant Governor Mark Taylor to bring more jobs into the state's rural, economically depressed areas.

> *What we found, particularly in rural areas, was a shortage of rental properties, of single family starter homes for sale and of land available for building, all of which can impact whether a company chooses to build in a particular location.*

—Dr. Tom Rodgers, Associate Dean for Public Service and Outreach

2001 – FACS partners with the Office of Public Service and Outreach to launch a "Latino Initiative" to help address some of the many challenges facing the state's growing Latino population in attempting to become part of Georgia's society and communities. Dr. Jorge Atiles of the Department of Housing and Consumer Economics is a champion of the effort. Study abroad programs are offered in Xalapa and Oaxaca, Mexico. Studies focus on cultural awareness, marketplace economics, education, child and family issues, nutrition, child and maternal health, and learning about traditional Mexican textiles. Alumni and other donors establish endowment funds in the college to help support students' participation in study abroad programs.

FACS Llega a la Comunidad Latina

2002 – Five FACS students are among 27 UGA students to study in Ghana during the summer. Dr. Patricia Hunt-Hurst, associate professor of textiles, merchandising and interiors, serves as the FACS faculty member teaching a course on West African fabrics, dress, and adornment. All participants complete a second course on African Society and Culture during the four-week session.

2002 – Dean Sharon Y. Nickols is elected president of the American Association of Family and Consumer Sciences.

2002 – In collaboration with the Governor's Office of Consumer Affairs and the Internal Revenue Service, FACS Extension implemented the Consumer Financial Literacy Program (CFLP) in 11 southeast Georgia counties. CFLP staff provide free tax preparation service to more than 275 families. Today, it is known as the Volunteer Income Tax Assistance (VITA) program. Students majoring in financial planning participate.

2003 – In order to streamline administration responsibilities, districts of the Georgia Extension Service are reduced from five to four. Currently, district offices are located in Athens (NE), Griffin (NW), Statesboro, (SE), and Tifton (SW).

2003 – The Georgia Soft Goods Education Foundation donates $500,000 to the UGA Foundation, establishing a distinguished professorship at FACS. Charlie Gilbert, of the Department of Textiles, Merchandising and Interiors, is the first to hold the position. Between 2012 and 2017, the college gains six additional professorships from donors and from the UGA Athletic Association.

In many places, the Athletic Association is funded by academics. Here, athletics is helping academics. What's happening today is just so exciting, because not only professorships, but scholarships for students in need are being funded by athletics.

—Dr. Anne Sweaney,
Josiah Meigs Distinguished Teaching Professor and Professor Emerita
Reflecting on her time as a member of the UGA Athletic Association Board

2004 – The Institute on Human Development and Disability, together with the Governor's Council on Developmental Disabilities and the Georgia Advocacy Office, form the "Children's Freedom Initiative." The mission is to transition 44 children and youth from institutional care to permanent, loving families, and to ensure that going forward, no child will be institutionalized.

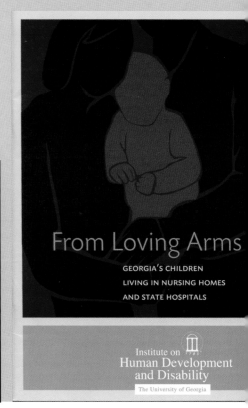

From Loving Arms

GEORGIA'S CHILDREN
LIVING IN NURSING HOMES
AND STATE HOSPITALS

Institute on
Human Development
and Disability
The University of Georgia

FACS FAST FACT
Student Organizations Supporting Professional Development in 2004:
- Alumni & Associates of Family, Career & Community Leaders of America
- American Association of Textile Chemists and Colorists
- Child & Family & Development Association
- Child & Family Development Graduate Student Organization
- Foods & Nutrition Graduate Student Organization
- International Interior Design Association
- National Association of Home Builders
- Phi Upsilon Omicron
- Student Association of Family & Consumer Sciences
- Student Dietetics Association
- Student Faculty Affairs Committee
- Student Merchandising Association

2004 – The Georgia Initiative for Community Housing (GICH) is started to help communities, large and small, improve the quality of life and economic vitality through the development of locally based housing and revitalization strategies. The Initiative grew out of Georgia's experience with the National League of Cities' Affordable Housing Program. Since 2005, sixty communities have directly benefitted from the program. Partners include the UGA Public Service and Outreach office, the Georgia Municipal Association, and the Georgia Department of Community Affairs.

2004 – Male enrollment in the college reaches 27 percent.

2005 – Five students complete the University of Georgia/Medical College of Georgia child life and family education program. Students pursuing this degree must complete over a thousand hours of clinical experience with hospitalized children and families. A Child Life workshop, developed in conjunction with Children's Healthcare of Atlanta–Egleston, is offered in 2007.

2005 – Dr. Don Bower, head of the Department of Child and Family Development (2005–2008), is elected president of the American Association of Family and Consumer Sciences.

2005 – The Department of Furnishings and Interiors moves to remodeled space in Barrow Hall. Drafting studios and state-of-the-art computer labs with AutoCAD and Adobe Creative Suite are now available for students and faculty.

2005 – FACS launches the first UGA Spanish-language website for students. Brochures related to foods and nutrition, housing issues, household toxins, and child care are also available in Spanish.

2005 – UGA officially launches the public phase of the "Archway to Excellence" fundraising campaign, with a goal of $500 million. FACS enlists the support of alumni, faculty, and external stakeholders to raise $2.6 million. Campaign goals include: 1) Building a New Learning Environment, 2) Maximizing Research Opportunities, 3) Competing in a Global Economy, and 4) Serving our Students.

"I feel that it is imperative that those of us in industry give back to the university and especially to the College of Family and Consumer Sciences. We must have graduates who have the intellectual skills to provide the innovation and leadership that our industry needs."

—Jeff Whalen, President, Georgia Soft Goods Education Foundation, Inc.

2006 – The family financial planning program is initiated. The program will teach students to become client-focused, professional, financial planners.

2006 – Despite the passage of child safety laws nationwide, use of child car seats in Georgia is only 80 percent. The Georgia Traffic Injury Prevention Institute of FACS offers educational programs designed to help prevent childhood injuries. The programs, offered through UGA Extension, reached 7.7 million Georgia residents. Child safety seats were distributed to residents in need.

2006 – The FACS "100 Legacies in the Making" campaign begins in March at the annual Alumni Luncheon. The goal of the program is to have one hundred households make a planned estate gift to FACS. At the conclusion of the program in 2008, 106 estate gifts were pledged.

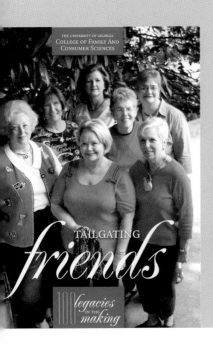

"There's really been nothing like it before or since, at the University. There was just lots of teamwork that went into it. The alumni got excited about it; everybody wanted to be a part of it."

—Katrina Bowers, Former FACS Director of Development

2006 – After serving 15 years as dean of the college, Sharon Y. Nickols "steps up" to the faculty of the Department of Housing and Consumer Economics. She continues to teach, conduct research, consult, and publish comprehensive works. Dr. Jan Hathcote serves as acting dean until August 2007.

2007 – Dr. Laura Dunn Jolly is named dean of FACS. She is known for actively embracing the interdisciplinary and integrative nature of family and consumer sciences. Jolly's mantra, "Focus, Believe, Laugh," continues to influence her day-to-day responsibilities as the dean of the College of Human Sciences at Iowa State University.

2007 – The Centers for Disease Control and Prevention awards the Institute on Human Development and Disability (IHDD) a $1.1 million grant to research methods to prevent injuries among youth involved in agriculture. More than a hundred children are killed and 26,000 are seriously injured in farm-related accidents each year in the United States.

2007 – In an effort to provide comprehensive programming to residents across all counties in the state, the UGA Extension Service rolls out the "40 Gallon Challenge" to teach residents how to conserve water and the "Walk Georgia" program, which promotes a healthy lifestyle through exercise.

2007 – Beverly Sparks becomes the first woman to head the UGA Extension Service as associate dean of the College of Agricultural and Environmental Sciences. "I'm proud to know we are just as important now as we were in the past," Sparks said on the occasion of her retirement in 2014. "There are always going to be new problems, and our relevance is still there. We have new agents that learn in different ways, and they will teach in different ways."

FACS FAST FACT
Enrollment:
    1990 – 530 Students
    1991 – 824 Students
    1994 – 780 Students
    1998 – 1,108 Students
    2001 – 1,356 Students
    2004 – 1,706 Students

Read through the resume of Dr. James Walters and one of the first things you notice is the number of "firsts." First male in the United States to be appointed a family life extension specialist, first male home economics faculty member at Oklahoma A&M College (now Oklahoma State University), first male department head at the UGA College of Home Economics, and one of the first men to be honored by the American Home Economics Association (now American Association of Family and Consumer Sciences).

During his 40-year career, the last 15 of which were spent at UGA, Walters left an indelible mark on the field of family and consumer sciences. He was recognized numerous times for his contributions in the classroom, to research, and to scientific publications. Among his most cherished awards was being named a Josiah Meigs Distinguished Teaching Professor in 1984.

Accolades and achievements aside, what his resume fails to provide is a feel for Walters's sense of humor, the great mentors that helped shape his career, his commitment to his field, and perhaps most important, his complete command of the English language. In the book *Leaders in Family and Consumer Sciences* (published in 2016 by Kappa Omicron Nu, the National Honor Society for the Human Sciences), Walters's autobiographical submission reflects on his life, his career, and what he feels is the future of family and consumer sciences.

Influences on My Early Life

"My first knowledge of home economics was in junior high school. At that time, the girls were required to take a course in home economics, and the boys were required to take a course in industrial arts. We were being prepared for roles that were, it was generally believed, appropriate to our gender. There was, I recognized even then, something wrong with our notions of gender specificity."

Oklahoma A&M

"If we were inclined to believe that faculty in the old days had it made, I wish to tell you that our office hours were from 8:00 a.m. until 5:00 p.m., Monday through Friday, and from 8:00 a.m. to noon on Saturday. My nine-month salary was $3,680."

Florida State University

"It was very fortunate for me to have the head of the department, Dr. Ruth Connor, as my dissertation advisor. She was not only a meticulous editor with superb writing skills but she was willing to spend whatever time it took to help students achieve a high level of excellence in writing. I decided right then that as a teacher I would provide the level of constructive criticism that would make it possible for students to learn to write well so that their writing skills would not deter them from publishing in the leading journals in their field."

University of Georgia

"The level of scholarship today in the College of Family and Consumer Sciences is extraordinary. The philosophy within the college has been to attract the finest scholars possible and to create an environment where they can excel. I believe there is no program in which greater academic freedom exists. This splendid legacy has been continued under the leadership of Dean Sharon

Nickols. Faculty who are highly productive and competent, and have high regard for themselves, are not always easy or gentle, but they are wonderful for students. They are demanding yet highly supportive and provide superb role models. Graduates are truly advantaged by this legacy."

Following his retirement from UGA in 1989, Walters continued to serve on a number of master's and doctoral committees, and as the associate dean to Dean Nickols for six months. He describes this time as "an experience that makes me understand more clearly how fortunate all of us are to have talented administrators who are willing to take on these awesome jobs."

Our Future

It seems to me that our brightest future is found in staying true to who and what we are, translating the most relevant elements of our identity for the twenty-first century. The elements of our identity I consider to be more relevant are (a) the use of scholarship to solve daily living problems of individuals and families, (b) commitment to interdisciplinary scholarship and approaches to problem solving, (c) recognition of the role of human development in family functioning, and (d) recognition of the importance of community to quality of life."

A Personal Note

"Like many men of my age, my entrance into our profession was quite by chance, yet I cannot imagine being a part of any other profession that is of greater importance or could have brought me greater happiness. I am deeply grateful for the home economists, both women and men, who, in their search for ways to improve the quality of life, have contributed so richly to my understanding of myself and others and have truly made our world better."

CHAPTER 8

The "I"s Have It: Interdisciplinary, Innovative, and Inclusive

2008–2017

Not since the Great Depression has America experienced such a significant swing of the economic pendulum as it did for 18 months beginning in December 2007. Fueled by the failure of subprime mortgages—and subsequently, a global banking crisis—US gross domestic product (GDP) shrank during five consecutive quarters. It was not until the third quarter of 2009, with the help of an economic stimulus package, that the economy began to grow once again.

In a report presented by the UGA Terry College of Business to the Georgia Economic Outlook luncheon in December 2009, Georgia would feel the effects of the recession long after the start of the national recovery. Unemployment in the state stood at 10.2 percent in October of that year, with rural communities feeling the greatest impact. Unemployment would remain at high levels well into 2010. Recovery was characterized as "slow and bumpy." Manufacturing, construction, and the real estate market would begin to show signs of steady recovery in 2011. According to the Georgia Department of Labor, unemployment in the state stood at 4.7 percent in August 2017.

For many businesses and educational institutions, "doing more with less" became a recurring theme; it's one that resonates still today. The need for innovation, creativity, inclusion, and resiliency was never more clear. With decades of experience, the College of Family and Consumer Sciences has always known what it would take to move forward.

> *At the end of the day, we do have tough decisions to make, but I really do believe that we work better together and that's really important to me. We're seen as leading in a lot of ways, whether it's the student-centered approach we have or the collaborations that we have for research and teaching. I try to be very deliberate in thinking that there are other ideas and other people that we likely should bring to the table.*

—Dean Linda Kirk Fox

TIMELINE

2008 – The McPhaul Marriage and Family Therapy Clinic is renamed the ASPIRE Clinic. The new clinical concept, created by a collaborative group of FACS faculty, offers a unique environment where UGA students, faculty, staff, and residents of the surrounding communities can receive individual, couple, and family therapy, financial counseling and education, nutrition counseling and education, and legal-problem solving services.

2008 – Cost-saving measures are implemented campus-wide. One visible example is the 2008 FACS Annual Report. Though the same number of pages as in years past, the report is half the size due to printing on both sides of the paper.

2008 – The "Jennie Bell" is brought out of retirement as a temporary substitute for the UGA Chapel Bell that was damaged following a Bulldogs victory over Florida.

2008 – FACS Extension publishes and distributes 9,000 copies of the *Guide for New Parents*. The publication is distributed through 24 hospitals in 22 counties in Georgia. It provides new parents with research-based, relevant information about caring for newborns.

FACS FAST FACT

The rising cost of a college education for full-time undergraduate students per year. Includes tuition, room and board, fees, books and supplies, transportation, and personal expenses:

- 1924 – $478 *
- 2007 – $16,054
- 2011 – $20,820
- 2014 – $22,680
- 2016 – $26,208
  - *$6,843 in 2017 dollars

Guide for
New Parents
The University of Georgia Cooperative Extension • Family & Consumer Sciences

NURTURING your baby's brain

Breast and bottle **FEEDING TIPS**

Building **FAMILY RELATIONSHIPS**

Is your **BUDGET** ready for baby?

What to expect the FIRST MONTH

THINK SAFETY in your home & car

Finding quality CHILD CARE

www.gafamilies.org

2009 – The Family and Community Resilience Laboratory is established by Dr. Jay Mancini, head of the Department of Child and Family Development. The laboratory studies the effect of deployment on military families and the role of prevention and intervention in helping families adapt.

2009 – Construction of the AgrAbility Farm begins in November in Tifton. The groundbreaking facility utilizes the latest technology available to assist agricultural workers with disabilities. The project is a joint venture between the Institute on Human Development and Disability and Cooperative Extension, and is funded by the United States Department of Agriculture.

2009 – Dr. Suraj Sharma of FACS and Dr. K. C. Das from the College of Engineering begin an interdisciplinary partnership exploring the transformation of algae into useable bio-plastics and other materials.

2009 – The first group of TMI students travels to China for the study abroad program. Since 2009, the programs have grown from five locations to eight, and participation has increased more than 50 percent, from 75 students to 118 in 2016.

2009 – In an effort to reach new audiences for UGA Extension, the UGA GreenWay website is established. The information focuses on ways to live greener, healthier lives. Today, visitors to the site will also find a number of social media tools including Facebook, Twitter, Pinterest, and YouTube.

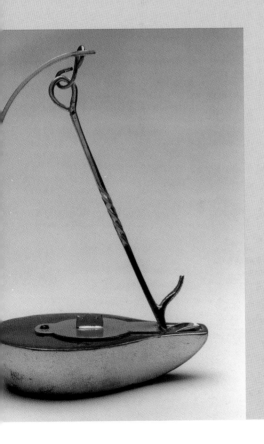

2010 – The American Association of Family and Consumer Sciences unveils an updated "Betty Lamp." The name, based on the German words "besser," or "bête," means "to make better." The lamp has served as the symbol of the organization since 1926.

2010 – Dr. Laura Jolly accepts the position of vice president of instruction for the university. Dr. Anne Sweaney is appointed acting dean in September.

2010 – FACS Computer Services becomes the Office of Technology and Instructional Services (OTIS). For nearly 30 years, the department has served FACS by providing leadership in the integration and use of technology throughout the college.

2010 – The FACS 2010–2020 Strategic Plan is established. Aligned with the seven goals established by the university, each goal has a series of benchmarks which inform the college's teaching, public service, and research activities.

1. Build on Excellence in Undergraduate Education
2. Build on Excellence in Graduate Education
3. Invest in Current and Emerging Areas of Research Excellence
4. Serve the Citizens of the State of Georgia
5. Improve Faculty and Staff Recruitment, Retention, and Development
6. Enhance the Physical and Technological Environment and Capabilities
7. Improve Stewardship of Natural Resources and Advance the College's Dedication to Sustainability

College of Family and Consumer Sciences
Strategic Plan
2010-2020
The University of Georgia

2010 – The Center for Undergraduate Research Opportunities (CURO) opens to all UGA undergraduate students, providing an opportunity to participate in faculty-mentored research projects. Since 2014, CURO Research Assistantships provide $1,000 stipends to 250 UGA students each year. In 2016, the number is increased to 500 students. Katalin Medvedev, associate professor of textiles, merchandising and interiors, and Richard Lewis, UGA Foundation professor of nutrition, are recognized by the university as outstanding mentors to students in the program.

2010 – Couture a la Cart, a mobile "pop-up" boutique, is funded by the James Family Foundation and launched by TMI lecturer Emily Blalock. "The goal of the pop-up boutique is students get to practice retail startup from the origin of the idea to implementation, pricing, selling, and marketing," Blalock told *FACS Magazine* in 2014. That same year, the boutique acquired wheels, allowing it to travel around campus selling merchandise designed and produced by students.

2011 – Dr. Linda Kirk Fox is named dean of the college in July. Prior to her appointment, she served as dean and director of Extension at Washington State University.

My job is to provide vision and a collaborative environment for administrators, faculty, staff, and students to succeed. In FACS, we are studying the sciences and applying the principles of business and design in the human sciences. I am a strong advocate for the integration of research, teaching, and public service to fulfill the land-grant university obligations to develop strong economics, safe and diverse communities, and healthy children and families.

—Dean Linda Kirk Fox

2011 – The UGA Alumni Association launches the "40 Under 40 Program," a campus-wide collaboration supported by the Division of Development and Alumni Relations, the Division of Student Affairs, and all academic departments. The annual recognition goes to graduates who have made significant impacts in business, leadership, community, and educational or philanthropic endeavors. Since 2011, 15 FACS graduates under the age of 40 have been honored.

THE UNIVERSITY OF GEORGIA

OFFICIAL TARTAN

College of Family and Consumer Sciences
Department of Textiles,
Merchandising and Interiors

2011 – FACS receives a red and black tartan design from UGA alumnus Walter Estes. The tartan is officially recognized by the Scottish Register of Tartans, Scotland's national repository for all tartan designs. Royalties from the sale of items featuring the tartan are used to support student scholarships and other services.

2011 – The University of Georgia commemorates its 50th anniversary of desegregation with a series of campus-wide events celebrating the courage of the pioneering students who broke the color barrier and those who supported them. A five-year diversity plan, "Embracing Diversity and Inclusion at UGA," is presented in August. The plan includes five goals that relate to institutional climate, recruitment and retention of diverse students, faculty, and staff, diversity-related research and program initiatives, and accountability.

Let the legacy of Hamilton Holmes, Charlayne Hunter and Mary Frances Early inspire us as students, faculty, staff and alumni to do all we can, collectively and individually, to continue to build a great university that celebrates diversity and provides a welcoming environment for all.

—Provost Jere W. Morehead
University of Georgia Diversity Plan,
2011–2016

2012 – The FACS Faculty Advisory Committee (FAC) begins development of a diversity plan. "Diversity and Inclusion – A FACS Plan for Action" is adopted in 2015. The plan, being implemented in phases from 2015 to 2018, is focused on five themes:

•Raise awareness and effectively support, recruit, and retain undergraduate and graduate students

•Enhance current and expand new curricula and student diversity experiences

•Raise awareness and support, recruit and retain faculty and staff, make policy and structural changes in the college, and develop partnerships between the college and other UGA diversity resources

•Create training and enhance educational outreach opportunities that reflect the college's values

•Increase internal and external communications of our commitment to the values of diversity and inclusion

I've had some opportunities through my leadership journey that took me to different places in the world. We spent two weeks in South Africa and that was in 1995, the year after Apartheid had ended. If you want to study leadership, we couldn't have been at a better, more interesting place in history. What I watched was the power of the population in inclusion and all voices at the table. I took away from that my feeling of organizational justice, justice within a college in how I work as a dean. I need a diverse set of department heads from expertise and experience, gender, ethnicity and bringing in voices. So I just think it makes a richer, more responsive, more dynamic approach.

—Dean Linda Kirk Fox

2012 – The UGA Obesity Initiative, involving several colleges and centers, is launched in January, led by Dr. Cliff Baile. The project combines obesity-related instruction and research activities with public service and outreach to develop obesity prevention and treatment programs for Georgia communities, employers, and healthcare providers. In 2017, Dr. Leann Birch, a leading obesity researcher and the William P. Flatt Professor in the Department of Foods and Nutrition, is named the new director.

College of Family and Consumer Sciences
UNIVERSITY OF GEORGIA

2012 – After extensive design, development, and input from faculty, staff, graduate students, FACS Ambassadors, and the Alumni Association's board of directors, a new FACS logo is launched in January.

A re-branding effort by the university in 2016 defined a new, unified look for all colleges and units, ending the use of individual college logos.

2012 – Eight online courses are developed across all FACS departments. Course offerings continue to expand to include degree programs. Two non-thesis master of science degree programs—in community nutrition and financial planning—are now available online.

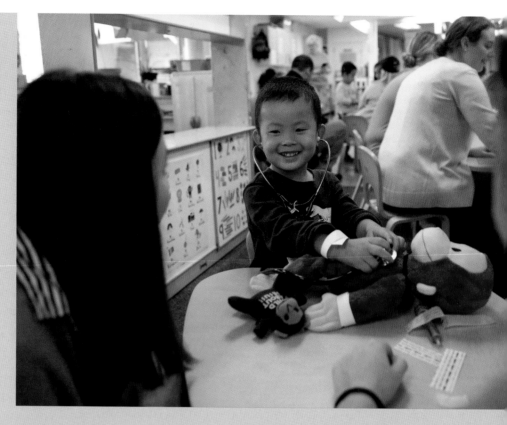

2012 – The Department of Child and Family Development becomes the Department of Human Development and Family Science.

2013 – More than 6,200 sessions are held by the FACS Public Service, Outreach, and Extension programs, reaching more than 155,000 Georgia residents.

2013 – The Department of Housing and Consumer Economics becomes the Department of Financial Planning, Housing, and Consumer Economics. The name change reflects the growing importance of the financial planning portion of the curriculum. In 2014, the department begins offering an online master's degree program. The non-thesis program prepares graduates to sit for the certified financial planner examination. In 2017, a new radio program, *Nothing Funny about Money*, is launched to help listeners answer an array of money-related questions.

2013 – Jere W. Morehead is named the 22nd president of the University of Georgia. Morehead had previously served as senior vice president for academic affairs and provost since 2010.

2013 – FACS joins the world of social media by establishing a Facebook page in November. This is quickly followed by a presence on Twitter, YouTube, Instagram, and the establishment of a Flickr account for the sharing of photo galleries.

2014 – Cooperative Extension across the nation celebrates a hundred years of the Smith-Lever Act. Throughout its history, the organization has provided unbiased, research-based information and programs to Georgia residents of all ages, in areas of agriculture, the environment, families, food, and lawn and garden care.

2014 – FACS graduate Bubba Watson wins the Masters Tournament at Augusta National Golf Club.

2014 – The "Squash Senior Hunger" Coalition is formed to promote food security among the area's senior population. The coalition is a cooperative effort among the UGA Department of Foods and Nutrition, the Office of Service-Learning, the Athens Community Council on Aging (ACCA), UGArden, and the Food Bank of Northeast Georgia. According to the National Council on Aging, more than 10 million older adults in the United States are at risk for hunger in 2014; Georgia is among the top 10 states for older adults at risk.

2014 – Sports nutrition becomes a new emphasis in the Department of Foods and Nutrition. Courses are taught in both spring and fall semesters.

2014 – The Office of Student Services becomes the Student Success and Advising Center. The focus is to improve the undergraduate student experience through innovative and integrated programs. Among the first initiatives to be launched is "The Bridge," helping first-year and transfer students navigate through the many challenges facing new students, including housing, nutrition, social networking, and money management.

2014 – The first students enroll in the new university-wide, interdisciplinary, graduate certificate program in obesity and weight management. This program prepares students to address the obesity epidemic in clinical, community, school, workplace, and research settings.

2015 – Thomas Davis, a 2011 consumer economics graduate and former All-American linebacker for the Bulldogs, is named the 2014 Walter Payton NFL Man of the Year. He is a linebacker for the Carolina Panthers. Off the field, Davis founded the Thomas Davis Defending Dreams Foundation (TDDDF), a nonprofit organization dedicated to providing programs that enhance the quality of life for underprivileged children and their families.

2015 – The first "Tiny House" class is held. Thirteen students, under the guidance of FACS assistant professor Kim Skobba and College of Agricultural and Environmental Sciences (CAES) associate professor David Berle, spend 16 weeks planning and building the 150-square-foot residence, complete with a working kitchen, a bathroom, a sleeping loft, and recreation and storage space.

2015 – The inaugural FACS Week is held to celebrate the FACS family and build a sense of community among alumni and friends.

2015 – The first Sweaney Innovation Award is given to Ann Woodyard, assistant professor of financial planning, housing and consumer economics. The award provides funds to support current faculty and students' projects and programs, as well as new programs that are created to meet emerging needs. With the award, Woodyard creates a highly impactful student experience within the FACS 2000E online course.

2015 – Governor Nathan Deal proclaims December 3 as the Family and Consumer Sciences "Dine-In Day in Georgia."

"*Family meals foster warmth, security, and love, and can be a unifying experience for all; and Family and Consumer Sciences professionals promote families eating and preparing meals together as a way to nurture strong family bonds and improve nutrition. Last year, more than 100,000 families committed to preparing and eating a healthy meal together on 'Dine-In' Day.*"

—Proclamation signed by Governor Nathan Deal, November 9, 2015

2016 – The Youth Obesity Undergraduate Research and Extension fellowship grant for undergraduate researchers is launched. The three-year grant, funded by the USDA National Institute for Food and Agriculture, aids in the development of childhood obesity intervention programs.

2016 – Formation of the Advanced Functional Fabrics of America (AFFOA) partnership is announced by the Department of Defense. Led by MIT, the partnership combines the knowledge and resources of national public and private entities to expand the use of fibers and textiles in military, industrial, and commercial applications.

FACS FAST FACT
Honor Hall Recipients, 2008–2017:
- Marian Chesnut McCullers
- Dr. Elizabeth Sheerer
- Dr. William Flatt
- Dr. Sharon Y. Nickols
- Louise James Hyers
- Dr. Anne Sweaney
- Dr. Gene Brody
- Dr. Josephine Martin
- Dr. Roy Martin
- Dr. Zolinda Stoneman

2017 – Five students are admitted into the inaugural Destination Dawgs program, a five-semester, inclusive post-secondary program open to young adults with developmental or intellectual disabilities. The program, part of the FACS Institute on Human Development and Disability, allows students to live on campus, audit classes, and have the support of a peer mentor to help improve their independent living skills. Students completing the program receive a certificate of completion.

2017 – Former Denver Broncos running back and 1994 FACS graduate Terrell Davis is inducted into the NFL Pro Football Hall of Fame. During his seven-year career, Davis led the league in rushing yards and touchdowns (1998) and was twice voted the AP NFL Offensive Player of the Year (1996, 1998). Davis retired from professional football in 2002.

Left to right: Katie Merritt, Britta Clark, Jordon Huffman, Chris Garrison, and Justin Majias

2017 – FACS adds Greece to its list of study abroad destinations. Students from FACS, and across UGA, experience an in-depth look at the causes, and aftermath, of Greece's recent financial crisis, including the current conditions and how consumers have been impacted.

2017 – The third annual FACS Week gets under way with the Homecoming Tailgate gathering on October 14 at Dawson Hall, just ahead of the UGA – Missouri football game. Other events during the week include "Dawgs with the Dean" and the third annual "Celebrating Excellence Lunch & Recognition Program." More than 275 student scholarship recipients, 20 faculty and staff, and 11 endowed professorships are recognized. The week also marks the 100-day countdown to the launch of the centennial celebration, which begins with a day of service on Martin Luther King, Jr. Day, January 15, 2018.

FACS FAST FACT

Enrollment:
2008 – 1,580 Students
2010 – 1,510 Students
2014 – 1,504 Students
2017 – 1,504 Students

Personal Journey – Drs. Gene Brody and Velma McBride Murry

For more than 20 years, the Department of Child and Family Development, through the Center for Family Research, has been conducting research of rural African American families in Georgia to identify family and community processes that predict academic, emotional, and behavioral success in children and adolescents living in conditions of environmental stress. Two of the champions of this extensive research are Drs. Gene Brody and Velma McBride Murry. Their work led to the creation of the Strong African American Families (SAAF) program, which works to strengthen the family unit and reduce the incidence of substance abuse and other high-risk behavior among rural African American families with adolescent children.

Early in his career, Dr. Brody's research was focused on the influence of parents' psychological functioning, parenting practices, and sibling relationships on the emotional and behavioral well-being of children and adolescents. Dr. Murry has done extensive research to identify the key factors that prevent emotional problems and risk-taking behavior among African American youth. It's no surprise that Brody and Murry's collaborative research would show that parents who get involved in their children's activities, both in school and out, and who have frequent, open family discussions, are raising children who are better equipped to handle today's challenges. "It doesn't take a rocket scientist to find out why things go wrong," Brody explained. "But we're trying to develop models of what promotes competence." Murry concurred, "We've been able to identify what makes a difference in children's lives because we ask questions about what's working."

In 2002, the first of 700 Georgia families participated in the SAAF program. The seven-week, culturally sensitive program is geared toward children, ages 10 to 14, and their parents or caregivers. In 2008, the program received a $3.4 million grant from the National Institute of Alcohol Abuse and Alcoholism.

Today, in addition to SAAF, there's SAAF-T, which is specifically tailored for teens aged 14 to 16. The program focuses on strategies that help teens make positive decisions regarding their future while addressing risks that can stand in the way of positive development, including a focus on minimizing sexual risk-taking.

"Children nowadays are a new breed. Even the best of parents have a hard time. The pull of the world is so strong, and kids are learning or hearing stuff so much younger. Parents are at their wits' end about what to do."

—Jacquelyn Bailey, Community Liaison and Session Leader

Many parents who have attended the programs have made behavioral changes that are positively impacting their children.

"I learned ways to be a better listener and not to jump to conclusions too quickly."

"I learned not to lose it all the time when my child comes to me for help with a problem that he is having."

"I now take into consideration that my daughter is becoming a teenager and she now has mood swings. I also know now that I must follow up with what I say."

"I learned how to discuss discrimination, sex, drugs, prejudice, and alcohol with my daughter openly."

"I learned how to really listen to my children more and not fly off the handle as quickly as I used to."

"If you are concerned about your child's future, then try to listen and understand their wants and needs, especially if it is something to really help them reach their goals, and to always stay strong."

"Patience really is a virtue."

CHAPTER 9

Our Centennial Celebration

2018

Two thousand eighteen is a year of celebration for the College of Family and Consumer Sciences at UGA. A solid foundation has been established; the framework on which the college is based will continue to be reinforced, redesigned, and renewed to meet the changing needs of students, both present and future.

TIMELINE

2018 – The FACS centennial celebration begins with the Athens Martin Luther King, Jr. Day of Service on January 15. Students, alumni, faculty, and staff participating in volunteer projects in Athens, and across the state, took to social media to share their experience, tagging their photos with the hashtag #FACS100.

- -

2018 – The FACS 100 Centennial Exhibit opens in the Special Collections Library located in the Richard E. Russell Building. *OPEN DOORS: 100 Years of Family and Consumer Sciences at UGA, A Century of Growth and Innovation Built on the Principle of Public Service* contains photographs, articles, historic costumes, and artifacts spanning one hundred years of home economics at the University of Georgia. The exhibit runs through mid-May.

2018 – The Winter Cooperative Extension Conference, held at the Rock Eagle 4-H Center, celebrates FACS 100. The theme of the conference, "Collaborate to Innovate, Serving Georgia Together," symbolizes the close relationship between FACS and UGA Extension.

2018 – FACS Day at the Capitol celebrates the 35th anniversary of the Legislative Aide Internship Program, established in 1983. Dean Linda Kirk Fox is presented with a special proclamation, read in both the state house and senate: "I, Nathan Deal, Governor of the State of Georgia, do hereby proclaim February 13, 2018, as Family and Consumer Sciences Day in Georgia and recognize the University of Georgia College of Family and Consumer Sciences on the occasion of its centennial anniversary."

2018 – In celebration of the official anniversary of the college, February 23 is designated FACS 100: Day of Giving. Funds raised this day go toward the FACS Centennial Endowment for Student Success. This fund provides student support in the areas of leadership, travel, professional development, and other activities designed to enhance the learning experience for FACS students.

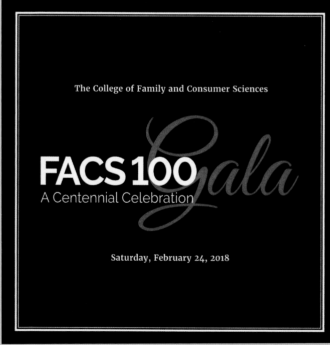

The College of Family and Consumer Sciences

FACS 100 *Gala*
A Centennial Celebration

Saturday, February 24, 2018

2018 – More than 500 alumni, faculty, staff, family, and friends gather on February 24 at the Athens Classic Center for the FACS 100 Centennial Gala. University of Georgia president Jere W. Morehead is the keynote speaker. Among those attending are six Honor Hall of Recognition recipients.

UGA president Jere W. Morehead congratulates FACS on its centennial.

Honor Hall of Recognition attendees (left to right) Zolinda Stoneman, Wanda Grogan, Bill Flatt, Louise Hyers, Anne Sweaney, and Sharon Nickols.

Another highlight of the evening is recognition of the FACS 100 Centennial Honorees, a prestigious group of influential leaders who embody the conviction and commitment to the ideals of the college, and who, through their vision and hard work, have been instrumental in advancing the college's ability to serve students and enrich lives throughout the last hundred years. Nearly 70 of the honorees, or their representatives, were on hand for the evening's festivities.

FACS FAST FACT

FACS 100 Centennial Honorees

Carolyn Ainslie • Jeanne Allen • Elizabeth Andress • Patricia Annis • Clifton Baile • Stella Bailey • Wanda Barrs • Carolyn Berdanier • Jenna Black • Emily Blalock • Jose Blanco • Julia Bland • Don Bower • Katrina Little Bowers • Wayne Brantley • Fanny Lee Brooke • Susan Hale Brooks • Zena Costa Brown • Thomas E. Cochran • Harrileen Jones Conner • Caree Jackson Cotwright • Constance Crawley • Aleene Cross • Brenda Cude • Leslie Greer Curl • Ilene Dailey • Thomas A. Davis • Kelly McGill Dean • William H. Elliott • Richard C. Endsley • Betty Etters • Nolan Etters • Joan Fischer • Megan R. Ford • Linda Kirk Fox • Jerry E. Gale • Charles Gilbert • Tammy Tate Gilland • Joseph Goetz • Jennifer Gonyea • Beverly Gray • Arthur Grider • Barbara Grossman • Earl and Anne Haltiwanger • Charles Halverson • Doe Harden • Ian Russell Hardin • Tonya Dalton Harris • Judy Ann Harrison • Grace Hartley • Jan Montgomery Hathcote • Judy Ellis Hibbs • M. Louise Hill • Patricia Hunt-Hurst • Kenneth Neal Ivory • Alisa Gipson Jarvis • Mary Ann Johnson • Laura Dunn Jolly • Lenna Gertrude Judd • Camille Kesler • Melissa Landers-Potts • Daisey Lewis • Richard D. Lewis • Charlotte Harris Lucas • Winnie Luffman • Estoria Maddux • Sara B. Marcketti • Dawn Brown Martin • Donna Schleicher Martin • Catherine McClure • Tommie N. Mullis • Rebecca McNeill Mullis • Emmie Nelson • Sharon M. Nickols-Richardson • Kathy Stephens Palmer • Lance Palmer • Theresa Perenich • Bonnie Stephens Petersen • Deborah Phillips • Cherish Farris Pinson • Marilyn LeCroy Poole • Sharon J. Price • Betty Sewell Ragland • Connie W. Rash • Jane Otwell Rhoden • Ava D. Rodgers • Thomas F. Rodgers • Cara Winston Simmons • Edie Edwards Smith • Daniel W. Stewart • Vera F. Stewart • Lynda Cowart Talmadge • John Hudson Taylor • Jim Thompson • Nayda Torres • Virginia Vickery • Kathleen Wages • Charlotte Wallinga • Lynda Henley Walters • Hines Ward

2018 – The centennial celebration continues with FACS Week, October 6–12. The Homecoming Tailgate party, Dogs with the Dean, and the Celebrating Excellence Luncheon are among the commemorative events.

2018 – On October 15, the college celebrates the birthday of Mary Creswell, the first woman to receive a baccalaureate degree from the University of Georgia and the first dean of the School of Home Economics.

Dedicated to a Strong Future

"As UGA continues to enhance the learning environment for our students, as we expand the research enterprise to solve the grand challenges of our time, and as we carry out our critical land-grant mission, the College of Family and Consumer Sciences will continue to play a vital role in our success."

—Jere W. Morehead, UGA President

"When you look at the human ecology model and you look at the mission of the College of Family and Consumer Sciences, I don't know of a major that is more diverse, more relevant, and that is more applicable to today's environment."

—Dr. Debbie Redeker Phillips

"In the future, family and consumer sciences programs have the potential for being the strongest ever. Our understanding of the myriad of problems faced by individuals and families is greatly enhanced by research and our historical interest in applying knowledge to solve problems."

—Dr. James Walters

"I think this next hundred years, the other colleges on campus will appreciate family and consumer sciences more, and collaborate more, and see the need to tie FACS research to their research."

—Katrina Bowers

"I believe the most important observation I can make as the first PhD graduate of the college, is to recognize that the philosophy and thoughtfulness of those who came before us is a legacy we pass on to those who will succeed us. The commitment to scholarship, to high-quality education, and to the support of students is both the history and the future of this college. It attracts those who share this vision and it is a powerful daily reminder of what we are about. As popular theories of higher education come and go, it will sustain us, and the college and those who are part of it will continue to flourish."

—Dr. Lynda Henley Walters

"Our college's next 100 years is our responsibility. It is our time to be brave and persevere. One hundred years from tonight, in the year 2118, I want whoever is standing at the podium to say the College of Family and Consumer Sciences is still helping students learn, grow, and contribute. That will only happen if we all make the commitment to get involved. Today, let's leave here proud of our past, inspired about our future, and committed to helping future generations learn, grow, and contribute."

—Tammy Gilland
Former FACS Alumni Association President

"I'm gratified to think that much of what we do in human development and family science is based on the relationship between two people, whether it's a family therapy program or parenting education program. I see that as continuing to be important, that we prepare people to understand the relationship aspect of what it's going to take to be effective in whatever role they play."

—Dr. Don Bower

"Whatever it is, you need to find your passion, something that you really believe in, and take the knowledge that you've gained here at the university and just do it."

—Dr. Anne Sweaney

"I think that what we have been doing for decades in the college, and will continue to do into the future, has such value and purpose that people really should know and appreciate it because one, it's applied, and second, that the students, through our degree programs, are so well-positioned with both subject matter content and an entrepreneurial spirit that we will no longer be a best-kept secret."

—Dean Linda Kirk Fox

References

1890 Universities. "The Morrill Acts of 1862 and 1890." http://1890universities.org/history.

American Association of Family and Consumer Sciences. "About Us." http://www.aafcs.org/AboutUs/index.

Anne L. Sweaney collection. UA11-202, University Archives, Hargrett Rare Book and Manuscript Library, The University of Georgia Libraries.

Bae, Jin Yung, et al. "Child Passenger Safety Laws in the United States, 1978–2010: Policy Diffusion in the Absence of Strong Federal Intervention." *Social Science & Medicine* 100 (2014): 30–37. Internet. Accessed September 13, 2017.

Baildon, Katherine, and Sarina Kumar. "The Special Milk Program: An Introduction." Cornell Center for Behavioral Economics in Child Nutrition Programs. http://articles.extension.org/pages/68764/the-special-milk-program:-an-introduction.

Carson, Clayborne. "American Civil Rights Movement." Accessed June 22, 2017. https://www.britannica.com/event/American-civil-rights-movement.

College of Agricultural and Environmental Sciences, University of Georgia. "A Short History of Wahsega 4-H Center." http://www.wahsega4h.org/history.html.

College of Agricultural and Environmental Sciences, University of Georgia. Georgia 4-H. "History of 4-H." http://www.georgia4h.org/public/more/history/nationalhistory/default.htm.

College of Agricultural and Environmental Sciences, University of Georgia. "Rock Eagle 4-H Center, About Us." http://rockeagle4h.org/about.html#history.

College of Family and Consumer Sciences, University of Georgia. http://www.fcs.uga.edu.

College of Family and Consumer Sciences, University of Georgia. Historical files and student scrapbooks, UA0054, University Archives, Hargrett Rare Book and Manuscript Library, The University of Georgia Libraries.

College of Family and Consumer Sciences, University of Georgia. Records, UA06-174, University Archives, Hargrett Rare Book and Manuscript Library, The University of Georgia Libraries.

College of Family and Consumer Sciences, University of Georgia. *Annual Reports*. 1991–2016.

College of Family and Consumer Sciences, University of Georgia. *FACS Magazine*. Fall 1999–Fall 2017.

College of Family and Consumer Sciences Alumni Association, University of Georgia. *Development Highlights*. 1996.

College of Family and Consumer Sciences Alumni Association, University of Georgia. *Highlights*. Summer/Fall 1993, Winter/Spring 1994, Summer/Fall 1994, Winter/Spring 1995, Summer/Fall 1995, Summer 1996, Winter/Spring 1998.

Cook, James F. "Cocking Affair." *New Georgia Encyclopedia*. November 8, 2013. Internet. Accessed July 18, 2017.

Darby, Matthew, and Aisha Yaqoob. "Disability Rights Movement." *New Georgia Encyclopedia*. January 4, 2017. Internet. Accessed August 10, 2017.

Dendy, Larry B. *Through the Arch: An Illustrated Guide to the University of Georgia Campus*. Athens: University of Georgia Press, 2013.

Editors of *Encyclopedia Britannica*. "New Deal." July 20, 2017. https://www.britannica.com/event/New-Deal.

Foner, Eric, and John A. Garraty. *The Reader's Companion to American History*. Boston: Houghton Mifflin Harcourt Publishing Company, 1991.

Georgia Cooperative Extension Service pictures, MS 2009. Hargrett Rare Book and Manuscript Library, The University of Georgia Libraries.

Georgia Council on Developmental Disabilities. "Impact Sheet." https://gcdd.org/.

Georgia Head Start Association. "History." http://georgiaheadstart.org/about/history.php.

Hatfield, Edward A. "World War II in Georgia." *New Georgia Encyclopedia*. December 23, 2016. Internet. Accessed July 18, 2017.

Henderson, Harold P. "Ellis Arnall (1907–1992)." *New Georgia Encyclopedia*. July 19, 2017. Internet. Accessed July 31, 2017.

"Home Economics." *International Encyclopedia of Marriage and Family*. Encyclopedia.com. Accessed July 31, 2017.

Hoover, Herbert. "Radio Address to the Nation on Unemployment Relief." October 18, 1931. Online by Gerhard Peters and John T. Woolley. The American Presidency Project. http://www.presidency.ucsb.edu/ws/?pid=22855.

John F. Kennedy Presidential Library and Museum. "JFK and People with Intellectual Disabilities." https://www.jfklibrary.org/JFK/JFK-in-History/JFK-and-People-with-Intellectual-Disabilities.aspx.

Lee, John Michael, and Samaad Wes Keys. "Policy Brief, Report No. 3000-PB1." Association of Public and Land Grant Colleges, WEB, John Michael Lee, Ph.D. and Samaad Wes Keys, September 2013.

Lyford, Carrie. *A Study of Home Economics Education in Teaching Institutions for Negroes*. Federal Board for Vocational Education, Washington, D.C.: Government Printing Office, 1923.

Mary Ethel Creswell papers. UA0014, University Archives, Hargrett Rare Book and Manuscript Library, The University of Georgia Libraries.

McFadden, Joan, Ruth Ann Ball, and Lisa Wootton Booth. *Leaders in Family and Consumer Sciences*. Lansing, MI: Spartan Printing, 2016.

McIntyre, John R. "Overview Study of the Textile Industry in Georgia: Emerging Trends and Patterns." June 21, 1997. https://www.scheller.gatech.edu/centers-initiatives/ciber/projects/workingpaper/1997/mc_textile.pdf.

Mize, Jesse J. *The History of Home Economics at the University of Georgia*. Athens: Agee Publishers, Inc., 1985.

Montgomery, Rebecca. *The Politics of Education in the New South: Women and Reform in Georgia 1890-1930*. Baton Rouge: Louisiana State University Press, 2006.

National 4-H Mobilization Week. http://4-hhistorypreservation.com/History/WW-II_Support/#TOC-05.

National Bureau of Economic Research. www.nber.org.

National Council on Aging. "SNAP and Senior Hunger Facts." https://www.ncoa.org/news/resources-for-reporters/get-the-facts/senior-hunger-facts/.

New York State Administration. Museum of Disability History. "President Kennedy establishes the President's Panel on Mental Retardation." February 26, 2014. http://museumofdisability.org/timeline/president-kennedy-establishes-the-presidents-panel-on-mental-retardation/.

Nickols, Sharon Y., and Gina Gould Peek. "The Opening Wedge: Mary E. Creswell, Home Economics, and the University of Georgia." *Family and Consumer Sciences Research Journal*, 45, (2017): 363–376.

Nickols, Sharon Y., and Gwen Kay. *Remaking Home Economics: Resourcefulness and Innovation in Changing Times*. Athens: University of Georgia Press, 2015.

The People History. "1950s Appliances including Prices." http://www.thepeoplehistory.com/50selectrical.html.

Public Relations photographs. UA04-041, University Archives, Hargrett Rare Book and Manuscript Library, The University of Georgia Libraries.

The Red and Black. Various issues. http://gahistoricnewspapers.galileo.usg.edu.

Roosevelt, Franklin D. "Inaugural Address, March 4, 1933." In *The Public Papers of Franklin D. Roosevelt, Volume Two: The Year of Crisis, 1933*, edited by Samuel Rosenman, 11–16. New York: Random House, 1938.

Statista. "Washers and Dryers – Statistics and Facts." https://www.statista.com/topics/2186/washers-and-dryers/.

United Nations. "Short History of the Commission on the Status of Women." http://www.un.org/womenwatch/daw/CSW60YRS/CSWbriefhistory.pdf.

United States Department of Agriculture, Food and Nutrition Division. "National School Lunch Program: Participation and Lunches Served." https://www.fns.usda.gov/sites/default/files/pd/slsummar.pdf.

United States Department of Agriculture, Food and Nutrition Division. "National School Lunch Program (NSLP), Child Nutrition Act of 1966." Last published April 25, 2017. https://www.fns.usda.gov/nslp/history_6#child.

United Stated Department of Agriculture, National Institute of Food and Agriculture. "Hatch Act of 1887." https://nifa.usda.gov/program/hatch-act-1887.

United States Department of Health and Human Services, Children's Bureau. "Children's Bureau Timeline." https://cb100.acf.hhs.gov/childrens-bureau-timeline.

United States National Archives and Records Administration. "U.S. Military Fatal Casualties of the Korean War for Home-State-of-Record: Georgia." https://www.archives.gov/files/research/military/korean-war/casualty-lists/ga-alpha.pdf.

United States National Library of Medicine, National Institutes of Health. *The Bureau of Home Economics: Its History, Activities and Organizations* (p. 1169). Washington, D.C.: The Brookings Institution, 1930.

University of Georgia Center for Continuing Education and Hotel. "About the Georgia Center for Continuing Education & Hotel." http://www.georgiacenter.uga.edu/portal/about.

University of Georgia Extension. "Timeline." http://extension.uga.edu/about/our-history/timeline.html.

University of Georgia Institutional Research and Planning. UGA Fact Book. 2001, 2008–2016.

University of Kentucky, Office of Philanthropy and Alumni, Hall of Distinguished Alumni. "Pauline Park Wilson Knapp." https://alumni.ca.uky.edu/hoda/pauline-park-wilson-knapp.

Walters, James. *Decades of Progress – 1971–1991: A Tribute to Emily Quinn Pou.* Athens: Georgia Southern Press, 1991.

Wayne State University, Merrill Palmer Skillman Institute. "Our History." http://mpsi.wayne.edu/about/history.php.

Wayne State University, Walter P. Reuther Library. "Merrill-Palmer Institute: Dr. Pauline Park Wilson Knapp Records." http://reuther.wayne.edu/node/6889.

Woods, Richard, and Nancy Rice. "Facts and Figures 2014–2015: Georgia's School Nutrition Program." https://www.gadoe.org/Finance-and-Business-Operations/School-Nutrition/Documents/Administration/Facts_and_Figures_for_SY2015_Final.pdf.

Zainaldin, Jamil S. "Great Depression." *New Georgia Encyclopedia.* February 1, 2016. Internet. Accessed June 26, 2017.

Photograph Credits

Hargrett Rare Book and Manuscript Library, The University of Georgia Libraries, various images

University of Georgia College of Agricultural and Environmental Sciences, various images

University of Georgia College of Family and Consumer Sciences, online images, Flickr

Cal Powell, Director of Communications, UGA College of Family and Consumer Sciences, various images

University of Georgia Photographic Services, various images

Page 12, Original Corn Club – Courtesy of Georgia Archives, Vanishing Georgia Collection, new-129–83

Page 15, UGA Women Honoring WWI Soldiers – Courtesy of Georgia Archives, Vanishing Georgia Collection, clr142

Page 27, FDR Campaign Visit to Atlanta – Courtesy of Kenan Research Center at the Atlanta History Center, VIS.146.01.20

Page 35, Woman Scientist in Lab Coat – Courtesy of Magnolia Box

Page 39, Eugene Talmadge – Courtesy of Richard B. Russell Library for Political Research and Studies

Page 45, Katherine Newton at 1973 State Normal School Reunion – Courtesy of Georgia State Normal School Records, Box #3, Folder #89, Courtesy of the Heritage Room, Athens-Clarke County Library, Athens, Georgia

Page 47, GE It's a Promise – Courtesy of miSci, Museum of Innovation & Science

Page 59, Textile Research – Courtesy of Kenan Research Center at the Atlanta History Center, VIS.122.17.02

Page 61, Eunice Kennedy Shriver with First Special Olympics Participants – Courtesy of Special Olympics, Washington, DC

Page 86, School Lunch Program – Courtesy of Richard B. Russell Library for Political Research and Studies

Page 122, Bubba Watson Receives His Green Jacket – Andrew Davis Tucker, The Augusta Chronicle, Augusta.com

Index